A WITTY
GUIDE TO
GROWTH MINDSET
FOR
TEENS

TRANSFORM YOUR THINKING TO UNLEASH YOUR TRUE POTENTIAL - SPARK RESILIENCE AND SUCCESS IN HIGH SCHOOL & BEYOND

Emma Davis

Impact
— PUBLISHING —

TABLE OF CONTENT

This page has been intentionally left blank

INTRODUCTION

"The growth mindset says all of these things can be developed. All kids need to do is try - put in effort - and they can get smarter, more skilled, and more confident."

-Bill Gates

HAVE YOU EVER wondered why some people seem to thrive despite facing challenges while others crumble under pressure? The answer lies in their mindset. A growth-oriented mindset is a powerful tool that can transform your life and help you reach your full potential.

As a teenager, you are experiencing a lot of changes in your life, such as hormonal fluctuations, academic pressures, and social expectations. In the face of these transitions, feeling overwhelmed and uncertain about your future is normal. However, it's important to remember that this is just a phase of life and that you have the strength and resilience to overcome any challenge that comes your way.

Many kids feel lost, doubtful, and confused during difficult times. Changes in hormones, academics, and social expectations can quickly cause stress and anxiety; you may feel lost during this phase of life. Life can seem frightening, with obstacles in the journey and no clear path ahead.

It's crucial to remember that this tough time is just a short phase of life's journey. Like a storm, it may feel overwhelming at first, but it will pass, leaving calmer waters and clearer skies. Now is the time for growth and discovery. You can experiment, uncover your passions, and create your path based on your situation.

As you approach puberty, feeling anxious or uncertain is normal, but always remember your strengths. Like a strong oak tree with deep roots, you can survive the hardest storms and thrive, as every challenge is a step toward adulthood, not a roadblock. Try to look at these issues as solvable and consider them opportunities to develop and learn. Remember that challenges can make you who you are meant to be. Every setback, failure, and doubt teaches you about yourself and the world; this will improve your long-term resilience.

One of the most common struggles for teenagers is self-doubt, which can affect their confidence and decision-making abilities. It's important to recognize that it's okay to make mistakes and not have all the answers. Seeking guidance from trusted adults or peers can help them gain perspective and build their confidence.

Another challenge that teenagers face is staying motivated and focused on their goals. It's easy to get distracted by social media, friends, or other activities, but it's important to prioritize your responsibilities and commitments. Setting small goals for yourself can help you stay on track and build momentum toward achieving your larger goals.

A growth mindset holds that hard work, perseverance, and persistence can develop intelligence and skills, which are the igniting factors that eventually help you succeed in whatever mission you are pursuing. A growth mentality believes our talents and gifts can be developed and improved, while a fixed mindset believes they are fixed.

There are various stories of famous people around the globe who experienced a positive change in their lives after implementing a growth mindset trick, which drastically changed their lives.

Michael Jordan's Determination

Many consider Michael Jordan one of the best basketball players ever, yet he had many experiences early on in his life that could have made him lose his passion. Jordan didn't allow not making the high school basketball team to stop him from success, as he kept working hard and doing better than anyone else could ever do. It motivated him to work even harder and do so consistently for amazing results. His determination and growth mindset made him a six-time NBA champion and global sports hero, which is a huge achievement that has yet to be broken.

J.K. Rowling's Persistence

Before becoming famous for *Harry Potter*, J.K. Rowling had numerous manuscripts rejected by publishers, which was heartbreaking for her at the time. Due to all those rejections and back-to-back failures in life, she struggled with poverty and depression. Rowling kept pursuing her writing career, and she never gave up; she had a strong desire to keep going.

She overcame obstacles, improved, and succeeded with a growth attitude, which in this chapter mentions how important it is for a person to have a growth mindset. Her wonderful fictional stories have inspired millions of people worldwide; not only were her words famous before, but as the new generation has arrived, they also appreciate her work. This shows the success that she has achieved was because of pure hard work and talent. It also teaches us to keep going despite failures when others give up at that stage and do not go after what they want in life.

Thomas Edison's Approach to Failure

Thomas Edison is famous for the invention of the light bulb, but it was not an early success as he failed so many times in an attempt to make the right product. Sometimes, the number could be more manageable. When asked about his many failed light bulb attempts, Edison famously answered, "I have not failed; I have considered 10,000 ways this won't work for making a bulb." His constant optimism and readiness to learn from mistakes demonstrate how a growth mindset can overcome obstacles and achieve the unachievable.

Oprah Winfrey's Journey to Success

Oprah Winfrey pursued her passion for being a broadcaster despite several setbacks in her life, including being told she wasn't good enough for television. She succeeded by working hard, staying tough, and believing in herself despite the harsh words of the people behind her. She became an entertainment industry powerhouse by showing that a growth mentality can turn obstacles into opportunities that can change your life significantly.

Stephen Hawking's Intellectual Ability

Stephen Hawking was diagnosed with Amyotrophic Lateral Sclerosis (ALS) in his early childhood. Hawking continued his cosmology and theoretical physics research despite an incurable disease that made him consistently weak and strengthless. He worked hard and didn't let his physical difficulties stop him. This shows how a growth mentality may boost strength and determination and help achieve huge things in life despite an obvious issue one is facing.

Accepting a growth mindset can change our lives drastically. We may break down our self-imposed barriers and realize our most significant potential by changing how we see ourselves. Self-discovery requires awareness of our thoughts. Think, feel, and behave based on your mindset — how you see yourself, your skills, and the world. Our expectations, how we handle problems, and our lives are all affected by it.

Why adopt a growth mindset? What are the benefits, and how can it transform your life?

So, what exactly is a growth mindset, and how does it help you? It basically means that you believe in your ability to develop your skills, talents, and intelligence over time through hard work, dedication, and persistence. By having a growth mindset, you're not afraid of challenges or setbacks because you see them as opportunities to learn and grow. It's much better than having a fixed mindset, where you believe that your abilities and talents are predetermined and can't be changed.

Starting with a growth mindset removes the constraints of a fixed attitude. You unbutton your collar and stop thinking your abilities and intelligence are fixed. Instead, you view them as skills you can develop with practice. This perspective shift opens up new learning and growth opportunities, providing you the courage to face problems.

With a growth mindset, you recognize that your worth is founded on your willingness to learn and improve, not your triumphs or failures. You become more forgiving of yourself, seeing your defects and failures as opportunities to improve rather than reasons to feel awful. It can improve your connections with others and yourself. Growth-oriented people are more open to feedback. Other people are potential partners and help on your path to progress and self-discovery, and they are only sometimes your opponents or competitors. By fostering collaboration and help, a growth mindset can improve your relationships and life in many ways. This teamwork gives you more ideas, more help, and ideas from other people to do well, as their experience can be used to solve a particular problem collectively.

How can you build a growth mindset for maximum benefit? You must be ready to tackle challenges, persevere when things go wrong, and believe in your potential to learn and progress further in life at a good pace. You must continuously improve and leave your comfort zone to achieve your goals, which once seemed impossible without learning about positive thoughts and self-development. Perhaps most significantly, it means learning to be nice to yourself and understanding that failure is an opportunity to grow.

Finally, believe in your growth mindset and boundless potential. To reach your full potential and live a meaningful, purposeful life, you must perceive obstacles as opportunities, failures as steps forward, and setbacks as temporary issues. What are you waiting for? Pick growth and opportunity and see your life change instantly.

Once you apply these principles in your life, you will see how drastically your life changes with the smallest of changes in your thought process. There's a beautiful quote by Brian Tracy that encapsulates this teaching: *"Positive expectations are the mark of the superior personality."*

Always keep in mind that your dreams are important and achievable with hard work and dedication. Don't let self-doubt or a lack of motivation hold you back. You have the potential to accomplish great things and make a positive impact in the world. Don't worry; you don't have to keep battling your fears and self-doubt. This book is your solution to overcoming these challenges and gaining the confidence you need to tackle your work with ease. Just keep reading, and you'll be on your way to success in no time!

Even in my own life's journey, I experienced several stages in which I was a victim of self-doubt, which caused me to lose plenty of opportunities that could have been easily grabbed otherwise. I was filled with regret and wondered how to break the cycle of negativity that was holding me back from progressing in life.

During that dark phase, a glimmer of hope led me toward brighter possibilities. This light is the concept of a growth mindset, in which our abilities are not limited or fixed and are developed over time through effort and dedication.

As I delved further into the principles of a growth mindset, I discovered that I was beginning to look at my life differently. I understood that the negative feelings about the situation and the constant self-doubt were because of my own limiting beliefs. I understood that motivation could be practiced through practice and ultimate discipline and used only by the inner self anytime, anywhere. I also understood the beauty of failure during the process because it was a stepping stone to success rather than a stoppage in my capabilities to do certain things. As Michelle Obama says, *"Your success will be determined by your own confidence and fortitude."*

After unlocking the secret of life, I realized I had the power to transform my life at will. It was a profound realization that inspired me to share this secret with the world. I knew that I could make a real difference in people's lives by writing a book about it. That's exactly what I did. My hope is that this book will help you unlock the secrets of life and transform your life for the better.

In the upcoming chapters, you will find some applicable strategies, real-life examples, and valuable insights that will help you overcome any problem that comes your way. You will learn how to overcome your self-doubt and create a mindset that will help you challenge any problematic situation or fear in life.

This book can bring hope into your life by letting you know that you are not alone. Many people around the world face similar problems, and this knowledge can inspire you to keep going, even in the face of losses. A positive attitude is crucial for success, and no matter how tough the journey may seem, you have the power and bravery to overcome any obstacle. Break free from the fear of failure holding you back. Break that negativity and make a positive shift to uncover your entire potential because that's the only way you will reach your full potential. Are you ready for this exciting journey that will lead you to a significant transformation of self-belief and a boost of confidence in your life? The choice is yours!

In life, especially during your teenage years, problems might seem impossible to resolve, failures can be painful, and the future is unclear. Feeling fear, forecasting failure, and settling for mediocrity rather than excellence is easy. What if you could overcome these constraints, see problems as chances for progress, and reach your full potential? This is where the growth mindset comes in.

Growth-minded people see setbacks as stepping stones to success, which comes from a positive mindset. They perceive problems as chances to learn, grow, and improve for a better future. They know that failures are tiny obstacles that teach them how to succeed.

Persistence is one of the most significant benefits of a growth mentality. Growth-minded people persevere when presented with obstacles, either externally or internally. They firmly believe they can overcome challenges with work and dedication. They utilize failures as motivation since they know they're one step closer to their ambitions.

With a growth mindset, people control their lives by setting their minds to it and managing situations without fear. They realize they can control their fates instead of being passive observers like most people. They know their choices affect their future, so they take responsibility for steering their lives in their desired direction. This goal allows people to set objectives, follow their passions, and construct the ideal life they have always dreamt of.

Another growth mindset trait is setting ambitious goals that are challenging yet achievable. A growth mentality seeks excellence in all areas of life rather than sticking with mediocrity, which many people tend to choose because they are afraid of the failure that they may have when they think of trying something new.

They appreciate the value of setting ambitious yet achievable goals that push them beyond their comfort zones, which is the first step toward success. They stay focused, motivated, and driven to attain their desires by creating specific goals and breaking them down into achievable steps. Realizing one's potential is essential to having a growth mindset, as you can only push the limits if you know the limits within. People with a growth mindset believe they can improve their skills through hard work and practice, as it comes with time and determination. They embrace self-discovery and personal progress, recognizing excellence is a lifetime quest. Readers can reach their maximum potential and be their best by adopting a growth mindset.

A growth mentality makes people resilient, determined, and empowered, with optimism and confidence. It gives students the skills and mindset to overcome hurdles and reach their goals. It provides unlimited possibilities and chances through self-discovery and development.

I've mentored teens from diverse backgrounds for over ten years and have helped them thrive. My teenage struggles inspired me to help other teens through puberty because I didn't want others to face the problems that I encountered. Due to self-doubt, lack of ambition, and uncertainty about my future, I understand the issues kids confront daily, which could significantly harm their future.

I saw how a growth mindset might alter lives as a teen leader. Teens who were depressed and self-conscious are now confident and able to tackle any issue. I love helping them succeed, and knowing I helped them realize their potential also helps me do more good things for these types of causes, as it makes a difference in people's lives.

Besides mentoring kids, I have a Master's degree in Counseling with a concentration on Positive Psychology and Personal Growth. I learned about human behavior, motivations, and resilience through my own journey toward self-development. I also discovered evidence-based personal development and well-being programs that have benefited me throughout my life.

The basis of Positive Psychology, centers around focusing on talents and values for happiness and health. I've learned resilience, tenacity, self-efficacy, and a growth mindset to examine how people can stay positive and overcome obstacles. All those techniques, though they seemed small, played a huge role in developing a sense of positivity in me in everything that I see through my eyes. As a counselor and positive psychologist, I mentor kids using proven methods that have helped me, other successful people, and people who aspire to be great. I aim to help kids succeed by teaching them strength, growth, and goal-setting, which are critical elements of success for many legends around the globe.

My compassion for the teens I teach boosts my academic and professional qualifications as it allows me to practice gratitude in life and gives me an inner satisfaction that I am able to offer help. I listen, respect, and give them a safe space to talk about their issues, express themselves, and achieve their goals as a mentor.

I write to inspire kids to grow and reach their potential. In "A Witty Guide to Growth Mindset for Teens," I encourage teens to believe in themselves, solve challenges, and live a meaningful, passionate life.

My counseling, positive psychology background, and teen mentoring experience make me competent to write this book. I aim to provide you with a growth mentality to tackle puberty confidently, as it is a crucial age for a teenager to make or break. I will teach you how to succeed in all aspects of life and realize your potential.

Personal progress and self-discovery require awareness of our thoughts because we must know in our minds what we are willing to change in ourselves. We think, feel, and act based on our mindset — how we see ourselves, our skills, and the world. It shapes our expectations, how we manage problems, and our lives.

Are you ready to embark on a journey of self-discovery and transformation of your mind to a fresh mindset of growth and improvement? Let's dive into "A Witty Guide to Growth Mindset for Teens" and start cultivating a growth mindset today!

CHAPTER 1

Understanding the Growth Mindset

"The moment we believe that success is determined by an ingrained level of ability as opposed to resilience and hard work, we will be brittle in the face of adversity."

-Joshua Waitzkin

EVER WONDER HOW your way of thinking can unlock doors to endless growth and success? This chapter unravels the secrets of a growth mindset and explores its profound significance.

The concepts of fixed and growth mindsets reflect how individuals perceive intelligence, capability, and challenges. Fixed-mindset intellectuals believe their IQ controls their thinking and limits their ability to learn and succeed. They avoid challenges because they fear they may expose their shortcomings or fail, making them feel less competent.

In comparison, the growth mindset holds that intelligence and skills can be developed by hard work and commitment. This approach sees the brain as a living, growing object that continues improving over time. Some believe this because skills are valuable, but what matters is how you develop them through hard work and learning. Challenges are opportunities to grow and improve, not issues to avoid. People with a growth mentality look forward to hard work because they see it as an opportunity to learn and grow. Mindsets affect more than education and jobs, as rigid people miss opportunities to learn and progress because of their constraints. They may not fulfill their potential because they fear failure and are afraid to take risks. This behavior can result in a life of unmet hopes and misery. A growth mindset makes you more resilient, versatile, and proactive. People with a growth mindset may overcome obstacles, learn from them, and advance in their personal and professional lives in ways that seem impossible to those with a fixed perspective by seeing effort as a means to mastery and respecting persistence.

This mindset encourages people to strive for greatness because they believe they can accomplish practically anything with hard work and determination. The contrast between a fixed mentality and a growing mindset reveals how our ideas of intelligence and talent can affect our behavior. People with a growth mindset have several options. For instance, they can turn challenges into opportunities and focus on lifelong learning.

The Science Behind Growth Mindset

Neuroplasticity allows the brain to form new nerve connections throughout life. Having a growth mindset is an essential skill that allows us to effectively learn, adapt, and overcome challenges. Our brain's neuroplasticity is a vital factor that supports growth, which includes myelination, synaptic pruning, and neurogenesis. These processes strengthen neural connections in our brains and help us acquire new skills, retain information, and develop new ways of thinking. Furthermore, research has shown that neuroplasticity can improve our mental and social skills, leading to personal growth and development.

Fact Check: Research indicates that individuals with a growth mindset, compared to those with a fixed mindset, are more likely to persevere through challenges and ultimately achieve higher levels of success.

Myelination is crucial to neuronal path function during learning. The brain coats these nerve lines with myelin as we repeat or learn.

2

This strengthens these routes and speeds up **neuronal signaling.** Myelination improves brain speed and performance, so "practice makes it perfect."

Synaptic pruning is crucial to learning. This mechanism removes inefficient neuronal connections to make room for stronger, more efficient ones. The brain optimizes its resources through synaptic pruning. By deleting unnecessary links, the brain may focus on strengthening frequently used pathways. Neuroplasticity's "use it or lose it" rule for neuron change emphasizes the importance of active participation and practice to learn and grow. Neurogenesis, creating new neurons in specific brain regions, contradicts the idea that adult brains can't produce new cells. While neurogenesis is slower in adults than in children, it provides us hope for lifelong learning and brain flexibility. Actively thinking helps grow new neurons, which improves the way we learn and adapt.

Neuroplasticity research supports the growth mindset concept. It suggests that consistent hard work, repetition, and persistence can restructure the brain to enhance problem-solving skills, learn new abilities, and improve performance. This knowledge makes it easier for individuals to adapt and learn. In addition, it gives them the confidence to pursue their goals, knowing that their efforts can positively impact their brain's structure and function.

Tips for Developing a Growth Mindset

Developing a growth mindset alters how we view our skills and solve issues. It requires altering your view of aptitude and intelligence from static to one that rewards hard work, learning, and perseverance. Our brains may change and expand amazingly, making this a powerful transition. The steps below are critical to developing a growth mindset.

Set Learning-Oriented Goals Focused on Effort and Growth

Shift from performance-oriented goals (which emphasize results and skills) to learning-oriented goals (which emphasize process and effort). Learning-oriented goals involve improving, learning, and exceeding your current abilities. Instead of attempting to acquire the top grade, create a learning goal to fully understand a new concept or improve by practicing. This new goal-setting method emphasizes effort, strategy, and progress, which are all growth mindset traits.

Reward Hard Work and Attempts, Not Just Talent and Outcomes

People should be praised for their hard effort, plan, and tenacity, as well as their talent or results. When we reward hard work, we educate people that learning and growth are more essential than being "good" at something. This makes people with a fixed mindset less fearful of failure and more ready to take on and learn from tasks.

> *"I'm reflective only in the sense that I learn to move forward. I reflect with a purpose".*
>
> -Kobe Bryant

Shifting toward a growth mentality requires a proactive and mindful approach to perceiving our abilities and facing challenges. Here are specific, actionable tips that individuals can start applying to foster a growth mindset:

1. **Catch and Reframe Fixed Mindset Inner Dialogues:** A growth mentality requires awareness of your inner thought process, especially if you tend to have a fixed mindset. This can manifest as self-doubt or a negative outlook on learning and new tasks. With a growth mindset, notice these thoughts and change your thinking about them. If you think, "I'm not good at this," ask, "What am I missing?" or "How can I do this differently to get

4

better?" This habit affects your immediate response to challenges and your long-term approach to learning and understanding. It shapes the way you tackle obstacles, whether you see them as insurmountable walls or opportunities for growth.

2. **Set Learning-Oriented Goals Focused on Effort and Growth:** Goals provide many people with a growth mindset. Set goals that emphasize learning and hard work rather than results like a prize or a good grade. Goals like "I will practice every day for an hour to get better" or "I will learn three new things about this subject every week" emphasize growth and effort. Setting these goals teaches you to value growth and learning over results.

3. **Reward Attempts at Challenging Tasks, Not Just Outcomes:** Even if you don't know what will happen, thank yourself for the hard effort and courage it takes to face challenging jobs. This strategy shows that hard work and persistence are more significant than talent or rapid wins. To demonstrate your gratitude after a challenging task, do something you enjoy. This mindset helps you perceive issues as opportunities to learn and grow, not as obstacles.

4. **Seek Constructive Feedback:** Request feedback without viewing it as criticism or a test of your skills; consider it useful information for improvement. Remember that you will constantly improve from the feedback you receive. Which steps can you take? A growth mindset emphasizes that skills and talents can be enhanced with practice and feedback; hence, being receptive to feedback is crucial.

"Trust in dreams, for in them is hidden the gate to eternity."

- Khalil Gibran

5. **Celebrate Learning, Not Just Achievement:** Celebrate both learning and the journey of pursuing your goal. Appreciate the new skills, knowledge, and concepts you learn. By perceiving learning as an ongoing journey, you support the growth mindset

belief that every experience is an opportunity to learn and better and that progress, not perfection, is the objective.

6. **Practice Persistence:** Develop a resilient attitude by persevering through tough times. Know that most good goals take time, effort, and tenacity, and if you fail, do not stop and keep practicing; eventually, you will succeed. Consider what went wrong when you failed, reflect on those mistakes, and figure out how to improve next time so that you do not repeat the same mistakes again. Remember that every attempt, even a failure, will improve your life.

7. **Cultivate Curiosity:** Curiosity characterizes growth; it inspires curiosity about new topics, ideas, and talents. Ask questions, try new things, and take advantage of learning opportunities, as curiosity makes learning exciting and opens you to new ideas.

8. **Surround Yourself with Growth-Minded Individuals:** The people you choose to spend time with can influence your attitude toward growth. Surround yourself with individuals who have a growth mindset and whose behavior you can emulate to foster your own growth.

9. **Reflect Regularly on Your Growth:** Regularly reflect on your personal and professional growth. Take time to journal your struggles, achievements, and lessons learned. This reflection allows you to see how you've evolved and emphasizes the importance of a growth mindset.

10. **Celebrate Effort, Not Just Talent:** Remember to recognize the effort and devotion that went into reaching goals, whether yours or someone else's. This supports the belief that success requires hard work and tenacity, not talent. Recognizing the importance of effort creates a more friendly, more supportive environment where growth is a goal everyone can achieve.

These habits can strengthen a growth mindset because they make you stronger and happier in life's trials and opportunities, both personally and professionally.

Key Takeaways

Growth Mindset Means Abilities Can Be Developed

The growth mentality holds that hard work and persistence can increase our skills, intelligence, and capacities. This mindset empowers people to tackle challenges, learn from mistakes, and strive for improvement.

Fixed Mindset Believes Abilities Are Static

Thinking that our skills are innate and unchangeable leads to feeling stuck. This perspective prevents growth by making people fearful of failure, avoiding difficulties, and believing hard work is meaningless without success. It makes learning and growing difficult, preventing people from attaining their full potential.

The growth mindset fosters ongoing personal development and growth throughout life. By believing we can change and improve, we may confidently tackle life's challenges, establish a lifelong passion for learning, and achieve seemingly impossible ambitions. Having a growth mentality can help you succeed in life and your career, and it shows how strong and flexible people are. To assess your current mindset and gain insights into whether you lean more toward a fixed or growth mindset, consider the following short quiz. Reflect honestly on your attitudes and responses to the statements below, choosing the option that best represents your typical reaction or belief.

Quiz: Assessing Your Mindset

For each statement, choose whether you agree or disagree.

1. Challenges are opportunities for growth.
- Agree
- Disagree

2. Intelligence is something very basic about you that you can't change much.
- Agree
- Disagree

3. No matter how intelligent you are, you can always learn and grow.
- Agree
- Disagree

4. You can learn new things, but you can't really change your basic intelligence.
- Agree
- Disagree

5. When I fail at something, it's an opportunity to learn and improve.
- Agree
- Disagree

6. Criticism is something you can learn from to improve your abilities.
- Agree
- Disagree

7. If you're not good at something, you might as well give up.
- Agree
- Disagree

8. Effort is the path to mastery.
- Agree
- Disagree

9. Your abilities are something you can develop through hard work.
- Agree
- Disagree

10. Talent alone creates success; without effort, talent is nothing.
- Agree
- Disagree

Scoring:
Agree = 2 points
Disagree = 1 point

Results

- 17 - 20 points: Your responses suggest a strong inclination toward a growth mindset. You likely see challenges as opportunities, value effort, and believe in the potential for personal development and learning.
- 12 - 16 points: You may have a mix of growth and fixed mindset attributes. Recognizing areas where you might hold fixed mindset views can help you shift toward more growth-oriented beliefs and behaviors.
- 8 - 11 points: Your responses lean more toward a fixed mindset, with a belief in static intelligence and abilities. Understanding a growth mentality can help you improve personally and professionally.

Remember that your mindset can change over time. How you handle challenges, feedback, and learning opportunities can influence your viewpoint. After learning about growth mindsets and how they work, we're almost ready to use them. Improving our talents and intelligence through dedication and effort is life-changing. From theory to action, in the next chapter, you'll learn growth mindset concepts, exercises, and real-life examples from us. We must shift our thinking about challenges and mistakes and respond to learning and improvement opportunities. We will discuss real-life growth mindset used in school, jobs, relationships, and self-care. The next chapter will teach you how to develop growth-oriented goals and build resilience to live with a growth mindset when things go wrong.

Follow these suggestions, and you will see genuine changes in solving problems, receiving feedback, and achieving goals. A growth mindset is personal and collective, impacting our achievement and how we influence others. Prepare for a life-changing journey beyond understanding growth mindset ideas. You will apply these principles to everything you do.

CHAPTER 2

Exploring Your Career Options

"The only limit to our realization of tomorrow will be our doubts of today."

                               -Franklin D. Roosevelt

A RE YOU STRUGGLING to find a suitable career and confused by the choices in the job market? No worries; this chapter will solve your problem and give you a suitable beginning in your professional career.

Overview of Different Career Paths

Choosing the right career is one of life's most difficult and important decisions. A single decision can either make or break your life as it shapes a person's legacy, helps them gain experience in a relevant field, and grows their career in the selected field.

The problem is that plenty of options are available, making it difficult for teens to make a choice. Below are a few of these options. See what suits you best.

1. **Health Care:** Health care is one of the most trending options for starting a career. It is famous for the potential of higher income than other professions and a social cause if you have the heart for helping others. Many healthcare jobs exist in various fields, such as

research labs, clinics, and hospitals.

Following are some of the essential jobs in this sector that might interest you:

- **Doctors** with advanced training identify and treat diseases. They may specialize in general medicine, pediatrics, surgery, psychiatry, obstetrics, or gynecology.
- **Nurses** collaborate with doctors to treat, monitor, and support patients. They may specialize in critical care, emergency medicine, oncology, and newborn care.
- **Pharmacists** are highly skilled and trusted medication experts. They understand everything there is to know about medications.
- **Medical Researchers** use science to discover novel disease treatments and cures. Universities, drug businesses, labs, and government agencies use them.

2. **IT Technology:** Technology and IT drive company growth, efficiency, and innovation in the digital age. Tech professionals can employ cutting-edge technologies and platforms in many ways. These roles matter are popular in this field:

   - **Software Development:** Software experts design, create, and maintain web, mobile, and corporate apps.
   - **Cybersecurity Experts:** These experts protect networks, systems, and data from hackers, viruses, and breaches by setting rules, implementing measures, and monitoring security risks.
   - **Data Analysts:** These analysts arrange and interpret data to help firms make wise decisions. They use statistics and data visualization to identify patterns and insights in massive datasets.
   - **IT Consultants:** These professionals help firms improve their systems and infrastructure. They may provide IT planning, project management, process optimization, or tech advice.

3. **Finance:** Financial and business environments are dynamic and competitive. People may grow and stabilize the economy in several ways, and the popular careers in this field include:

- **Finance Managers** spend, plan, and report on company funds. They study financial data, identify trends, and recommend strategies to increase earnings and efficiency.
- **Investment Bankers** assist companies in raising funds, merging, and conducting other financial arrangements. They advise customers on investments, finances, and negotiations.
- **Entrepreneurs** build firms and risk money to uncover chances. They create business concepts, raise funding, and expand their firms.
- **Marketers** target the correct customers to increase sales. They plan, campaign, and analyze customer and market trends.

4. **Academic:** Education shapes future generations and increases access to information and new ideas. You can teach, investigate, and aid others in this field by following the given professions:
   - **Elementary, middle, and high school instructors** teach various subjects and help young people grow intellectually and personally.
   - **University professors** teach, study, and publish academic papers. They also mentor graduate students and assist academics with conferences and articles.
   - **Institute directors** oversee colleges and universities. They make and enforce policies and oversee rules and budgets.
   - **Academic researchers** may use data, conduct experiments, and publish in academic publications for colleges, research centers, or government entities.

5. **Arts and Entertainment:** Arts and entertainment encompass various creative professions. These include film, music, theater, visual arts, and media creation. This job allows creativity and cultural enrichment. These essential entertainment and arts jobs include:
   - **Actors** who play roles on stage, screen, and television. They perform lines, convey emotions, and work with directors and other actors to create entertaining performances.

- Classical, jazz, rock, pop, country, blues, and hip-hop **musicians** write and perform music.
- **Writers** create stories, scripts, articles, poetry, and more by expressing emotions and ideas and captivating readers. They also collaborate with other creatives with novels, screenplays, news reports, and commercials.
- **Film, play, television, and musical directors** monitor innovation and artistic direction. They read screenplays, create visuals, and bring stories to life with actors, artists, and crew.
- **Set, costume, lighting, and graphic designers** enhance shows. They create sets, costumes, and other visuals to tell the story and engage the audience.
- **Producers** oversee finances, logistics, and development from planning to filming or performing to post-production. They finance, hire, manage budgets and schedules, and manage projects.

6. **Architecture:** Architects plan, create, and maintain infrastructures to aid in building houses, office buildings, and more. Popular engineering and construction jobs include:
   - **Engineers:** Civil engineering, mechanical engineering, and electrical engineering.

7. **Legal:** Lawyers protect rights, fairness, and compliance. Legal services include the following jobs:
   - Civil litigation, criminal defense, corporate, family, and intellectual property **lawyers** advise and represent clients. They produce court papers, represent clients in the courtroom, and negotiate settlements.
   - **Judges** preside over hearings and trials. They ensure the law is followed and provide fair, impartial, and legitimate court proceedings.
   - **Legal assistants, or paralegals,** assist lawyers with legal research, writing, case file organization, and court preparation.

- **Specialized legal experts** advise individuals, businesses, and organizations. Tax, labor, and rule-following guidance are available, helping complex case clients make sound legal decisions.

8. **Social Work:** Social professionals assist vulnerable individuals, address social concerns, and enhance communities and individuals. These roles matter in this field:
    - **Social workers** help with homelessness, mental illness, drug misuse, domestic violence, and child safety. They counsel, advocate and support people in tough situations.
    - **Mental health counselors** assist individuals, couples, families, and groups with emotional, behavioral, and social concerns. They evaluate clients, develop care programs, and guide them to healing and growth.
    - **Community organizers** empower and engage people and solve social concerns through joint action and advocacy. They organize and network for social justice, fairness, and positive change.
    - **Nonprofit leaders** run NGOs. They raise money, create programs, manage volunteers, and promote various causes.
    - **Environmental research,** conservation, green energy, and sustainability jobs have expanded as people are concerned about climate change, environmental degradation, and resource shortages.

9. **Civil Servant:** Federal, state, and local government administrations and agencies play a vital role in policymaking, service delivery, and public interest. Popular government and public administration jobs include:
    - **Public policy analysts** investigate, analyze, and evaluate government policies and programs for continuous improvement. They advise policymakers on facts for the government, study groups, advocacy groups, and consulting corporations.
    - **Diplomats** develop relations, negotiate treaties, and address human rights, trade, economic cooperation, peace,

and safety. They facilitate international collaboration in embassies, consulates, and groups.

- **Public health practitioners** improve community health through promotion, prevention, and education. They are also responsible for public health regulations, disease transmission research, and disaster planning.
- **International relations experts** evaluate global politics, economy, and social issues. They advise governments, businesses, and organizations on trade, security, development, and diplomacy. Their work in think tanks, government agencies, multinationals, and international groupings helps them rule on different matters.

If any of the above jobs interest you, take some time to research them. You can easily turn one of these jobs into a successful professional career.

Are There Wrong or Right Careers?

The question of a "wrong" or "right" career is complex and encompasses personal values, cultural expectations, economic concerns, and professional happiness. Some believe some jobs are ethically superior to others, but what's right or wrong depends on the person and situation.

First, let's define the "wrong" job. Many believe that working in businesses like firearms and tobacco is immoral since it can harm people, communities, and the environment.

Some jobs that lie, manipulate, or exploit weak individuals are immoral. Scammers, fraudsters, and sellers transgress moral and legal laws, and society criticizes them.

People argue that working for money or status is immoral without considering how it will influence society or your happiness. This opinion holds that prioritizing money or social prestige over contributing to the common good may lead to moral decay.

The "right" employment concept also implies moral absoluteness that may not fully express human complexity. Socioeconomic background, schools, personal interests, talents, and life experiences all influence employment choices.

People's values, priorities, and aspirations may change, causing them to reassess their career routes and make various choices. What was once the "right" job may not fit current ideals and aspirations.

Whether some jobs are "wrong" or "right" is subjective and multifaceted. Some jobs are unethical or bad for society. However, the "right" work depends on each person's principles,

Take A Break!

Need a quick stress buster as you might be tired of reading continuously? Dive into laughter! Spend 5 minutes watching hilarious videos or scrolling through funny memes.

Count every giggle, chortle, or belly laugh out loud. Embrace the ridiculousness and let yourself be silly!

Laughter not only boosts your mood but also lowers stress hormones and enhances overall health. Give it a shot now and share how many laughs you rack up!

societal norms, and personal fulfillment. People should consider their values, passions, and ambitions rather than morality when making career decisions. They should also align their professional aspirations with their values. Choosing a meaningful and happy career requires self-reflection, insight, and a commitment to morality and society.

Insights from Successful Leaders

Successful leaders can teach aspiring individuals a lot as they share particularities, events, and perspectives that have made them successful. They display resilience and tenacity when faced with obstacles. They usually fail on their route to success but view failures as opportunities to learn and improve. These leaders stay positive, bounce back from failures, and persevere to achieve long-term success. Success in any field requires networking. Successful professionals build good relationships with management, clients, customers, and peers. They actively foster trust, respect, and reciprocity. They use their networks to identify opportunities, seek advice, and collaborate. These leaders increase their impact and career prospects by developing meaningful contacts and building a supportive professional network.

Passion is a driving force for successful professionals. They are not just interested in their careers but passionate about them. This passion fuels their desire to help others, make a difference, and be creative. It aligns their career goals with their beliefs and motivates them to break the status quo and explore new methods of doing things. These leaders evolve, adapt, and outperform their competitors by fostering innovation through collaboration, diversity, and openness to new ideas.

Honesty and ethics are not just values, but they are crucial for a leader. Successful professionals model these traits, even in the face of moral dilemmas. They seek the respect of their co-workers, clients, customers, and others by sticking to their values. This commitment to honesty and ethics establishes trust, loyalty, and a strong work culture based on mutual respect and accountability.

Influential professionals who lead their areas can teach others how to succeed. Career-oriented individuals can achieve long-term success and satisfaction by embracing lifelong learning, creating solid relationships and networks, prioritizing purpose and passion, promoting innovation and creativity, and leading with honesty and integrity.

Choosing a Career Path

Career choice is a crucial decision in life as it influences your overall happiness. Choosing the right job might be intimidating, but it's essential to match your values and interests to long-term success. The following sections will describe the importance of knowing what you want, exploring job options, and making decisions that reflect your beliefs and aspirations.

Understanding Your Goals

Consider your hobbies, passions, and interests before accepting a job. Consider what makes you happy, motivated, and wanting to learn more. You can evaluate your skills from your strengths and weaknesses by asking yourself the questions given in the box:

If a job that best suits your personality comes to mind, pursue it after thoroughly evaluating your answers and asking yourself the given questions.

Discover Your Career Options

After determining your goals, do thorough research about the jobs that match your interests, talents, and values. Research different employment positions, sectors, and professions to learn about opportunities and the skills needed to succeed. Consider employment ambition, compensation possibilities, growth prospects, and work-life balance for the right decision in the long term.

Through networking and informational interviews, you can learn about job options and gain guidance from industry professionals. Ask successful people about their employment routes, experiences, and advice. Their career guidance can help you choose wisely.

Making Fact-Based Decisions

When considering a professional path, base your decision on your knowledge, skills, and interests. Think carefully about how each option fits your long-term objectives and values. Consider more than income or status; consider the job's nature, how you may advance, and how well it suits your personal and professional goals.

You can learn through volunteering and internships in companies as they offer hands-on experience, which will test your interests and skills.

19

These experiences can help you decide on a career path, build skills and contacts, and make sensible decisions.

As you progress in your career, remain open-minded and adaptable. Your goals and interests may evolve, allowing you to adjust your plan accordingly. Embrace the necessity of taking risks and learning from your mistakes to uncover new opportunities. Remember, career success is not always a linear path. Every experience, whether positive or negative, contributes to your growth. This reassurance should instill confidence in your career exploration.

> *"The minute you decide to do what you love to do, you have made a life plan for yourself and a career choice."*
>
> **-Huda Kattan**

Are you eager to take the next step toward your dream job? In the next chapter, we will plunge into making informed choices, overcoming obstacles, and finding a career that aligns with your passion. Get ready to absorb valuable information and receive guidance to enhance your job performance. Embark on the next phase of your career journey, filled with anticipation and excitement!

Key Takeaways

- Choose a profession that matches your values, interests, and goals.
- Learn about employment alternatives and skills by researching different jobs, sectors, and professions by researching.
- Consider your interests, values, talents, short-term and long-term goals while choosing a professional career.
- Find internships and volunteer opportunities to enhance your skills and network.
- Learn from failures and work toward continuous improvement.

Test Your Knowledge

1. What do you enjoy doing in your free time?
    a. Creating art or writing
    b. Solving puzzles or coding
    c. Volunteering or helping others

2. Which subjects did you excel in at school?
    a. Literature or art
    b. Math or computer science
    c. Social studies or psychology

3. What type of work environment do you prefer?
    a. Creative and flexible
    b. Tech-savvy and dynamic
    c. Supportive and collaborative

4. What motivates you the most?
    a. Expressing yourself creatively
    b. Solving complex problems
    c. Making a difference

5. How do you handle challenges?
    a. Embrace them as opportunities for creativity
    b. Approach them analytically and methodically
    c. Seek support from others and collaborate on solutions.

6. What kind of projects do you enjoy working on?
    a. Creative projects
    b. Technical or scientific projects
    c. Projects that benefit others or the community

7. Which job perk appeals to you the most?
 a. Creative freedom and autonomy
 b. Opportunities for innovation and advancement
 c. A sense of fulfillment and making a positive impact

8. What is your ultimate career goal?
 a. To inspire others through creativity
 b. To innovate and solve complex problems
 c. To contribute to the well-being of others

Results

- If your answers are mostly "A," you are best suited for a career in the arts or creative fields.
- If your answers are mostly "B," your skills and interests align well with careers in technology and innovation.
- If your answers are mostly "C," your compassion and desire to help others indicate a strong fit for careers in social services or healthcare.

CHAPTER 3

Reaching Your Goals with a Growth Mindset

"We are works in progress. The day you stop growing, stretching, learning, and expanding your mindset is the day your personal growth stops"

-**Kara Santos**

IMAGINE YOU'RE ON the brink of an opportunity that could lead you straight to your dreams. What's the key to turning your vision into reality at that moment? The answer is adopting a growth mindset and maintaining optimism about the future you envision for yourself. This chapter is designed to steer you toward growth, guiding you on a journey of self-development through embracing a growth mindset.

Are you prepared to transform your mindset from a fixed one to a growth-oriented one? By enhancing your mindset, you can unlock your hidden potential, anticipate any challenges that lie ahead, and brighten your future. It's time to learn about the adoption of a growth mindset and begin your journey toward it.

Adopting a Growth Mindset with Goals

The idea that skills can be improved is at the heart of having a growth attitude when trying to reach your goals. This view is very different from the fixed mindset, which says that abilities can't be changed. People who have a growth mindset, on the other hand, see their skills as changeable and know that they can keep improving with hard work, practice, and persistence. The growth mentality holds that abilities are flexible muscles that can be improved through practice and study. By viewing our goals this way, we can break free from our self-imposed constraints. We know that with hard effort and devotion, we can develop the abilities we need to succeed in our goals.

Weightlifters work hard to build their muscles and increase their strength so that they can lift heavier weights over time. Similarly, we can also train our minds to become more intelligent, innovative, and imaginative by consistently engaging in activities that challenge our cognitive abilities and expand our knowledge base. Just like weightlifting, mental training requires patience, persistence, and discipline to achieve long-term results. By getting out of our comfort zones and immersing ourselves in difficult tasks, we improve at many things.

Believing You Can Get Smarter or Further Develop Skills Over Time

Understanding that knowledge and skills can be increased through hard work and practice is crucial to the growth mentality, as this conviction motivates us to achieve great things and overcome challenges. Growth-oriented people perceive setbacks and issues as opportunities to grow and develop.

They don't let failures stop them or make them feel useless; rather, they believe they can progress with time. People who believe in their own improvement are more likely to practice and solve challenges actively.

Fact Check:
Carol Dweck's (2008) research suggests that having a growth mindset is associated with higher academic achievement. Success is not influenced by natural ability but rather by mindset and the desire to achieve one's highest potential and abilities.

Instead of being satisfied with their limited talents and knowledge, they seek ways to improve. People with a growth mindset strive to improve in new situations, learn new things, and improve their existing skills. This mindset also gives people hope and strength to overcome challenges. Rather than seeing defeat as a sign of weakness, they see it as part of learning. Each setback is an opportunity to learn, develop, and emerge stronger and more adept.

Problems don't overwhelm people with a growth mentality as they realize that hard work and dedication can lead to success. Believing in growth gives people the fortitude to take charge of their learning and work hard to achieve their goals. The growth mentality holds that people may improve over time. It inspires us to aim high and overcome obstacles by recognizing failures as opportunities to grow and believing in our potential to change; we empower ourselves to learn, adapt, and thrive.

Embracing Failures

Failure is part of a successful journey because difficulties will arise even with careful planning and hard work. How a person with a growth mentality handles failure distinguishes them from others as they view losing as a learning experience, not a reflection of their inferiority. Every setback, no matter how scary or gloomy, teaches us and helps us grow in the long run. Transforming failure into a learning experience can turn loss into strength, which is useful for tackling future challenges.

With a growth mindset, we can use failures as stepping stones to success, not as obstacles that hinder our growth. By adjusting our perspective on loss, we can create resilience — the ability to recover stronger and more determined. People learn from the things they lose and bad experiences, as loss is a detour that can lead to new opportunities and insights.

Breaking Down Big Goals

Making significant progress is both exciting and challenging, but a growth mindset can simplify the process by breaking down big goals into smaller, more achievable steps. With a growth mindset, you should focus on tiny milestones rather than the overall outcome while setting and planning goals.

Set Mini-Goals

Carol Dweck's (2008) research suggests that having a growth mindset is associated with higher academic achievement. Success is not influenced by natural ability but rather by mindset and the desire to achieve one's highest potential and abilities. One technique to handle enormous goals is to break them into smaller, more manageable "mini-goals." These mini-goals assist us in reaching the major goal and focus on acquiring the skills and information we need to succeed.

Breaking big ambitions into tiny pieces makes the journey less intimidating and more achievable. Each mini-target is a major step forward, providing us with a sense of accomplishment and keeping us continuing toward our main goal. Mastering one skill or job at a time can also boost our performance and success.

> *"There is always a step small enough from where we are to get us to where we want to be. If we take that small step, there's always another we can take, and eventually, a goal thought to be too far to reach becomes achievable."*
>
> **-Ellen Langer**

Measure Incremental Progress

As you pursue your goals, you must track your progress along the way, and you shouldn't just look at things such as sales or weight loss toward the end of reaching your goal. You should also examine process metrics, which track the actions and behaviors that produce those results.

You can track your daily progress and improve using process measures. If you want to write better, you might track your daily word count, draft revision time, and peer or teacher comments. Process metrics shift our focus from the end result to the actions and behaviors that make it happen as they improve our progress view and allow us to make sensible method improvements as needed.

Reward Small Wins

When we celebrate small victories, we set off positive feedback loops that keep us doing good things. Each step we take toward our goals makes us more determined to keep going. It is essential to break down big goals into smaller, easier-to-handle steps to become successful in the long run. We can develop a growth mindset that helps us reach our biggest dreams by setting small goals, using process metrics to track our progress, and praising ourselves for small wins that show how hard we've worked. We can meet any goal as long as we are dedicated, never give up, and keep working to get better all the time.

Overcoming Setbacks and Failures

Setbacks and blunders are inevitable as we pursue our dreams, and with a growth mindset, we may use these challenges to learn and grow. This section will discuss how someone with a growth mindset approaches setbacks and disappointments and how it can give us the endurance to persevere.

See Setbacks As Helpful Feedback

A growth mindset requires recognizing failures as opportunities to learn and develop better techniques. Unfortunately, issues and obstacles make individuals sad or furious, as it's innate human nature. However, these challenges are opportunities to learn and improve for those with a growth mindset.

When setbacks are seen as feedback, people can stay cheerful and focus on solutions. This perspective shift makes people more resilient and flexible, helping them recover stronger. People with a growth mindset analyze setbacks to determine what went wrong. They consider what went wrong, how to improve, and what to learn by self-reflecting, which helps them identify areas for improvement and adjust their strategy.

Accepting failures as feedback boosts responsibility and control. People who take responsibility for their actions and results, not luck or outside circumstances, help them regain control and overcome tough challenges ahead.

> *"Live the Life of Your Dreams When you start living the life of your dreams, there will always be obstacles, doubters, mistakes, and setbacks along the way. But with hard work, perseverance, and self-belief, there is no limit to what you can achieve."*
> **-Roy T. Bennett**

Use Failures as Opportunities

Embracing failure is essential for learning and growth. Recognizing failure as an opportunity rather than a sign of weakness enables individuals to develop resilience and strength. Here's how adopting a growth mindset can transform one's approach to setbacks and challenges:

- **Viewing Loss as a Temporary Setback:** People with a growth mindset perceive loss not as a permanent flaw but as a momentary challenge that can be overcome. This perspective encourages a focus on progress and learning, framing setbacks as opportunities for improvement.

- **Learning from Mistakes:** Instead of dwelling on disappointment, adopting a proactive approach to understanding what went wrong and learning from these mistakes is crucial. This process of reflection and adaptation facilitates personal evolution and improvement.
- **Building Resilience Through Challenges:** Every setback encountered is an opportunity to build resilience. By facing and overcoming obstacles, individuals become stronger and more determined, ready to tackle future challenges with increased vigor.
- **Persistence in the Face of Adversity:** Cultivating a growth mindset means persisting despite difficulties. Recognizing the importance of tenacity, individuals are more inclined to continue their efforts even when faced with setbacks.
- **Celebrating Progress:** It's important to acknowledge and celebrate progress, regardless of the outcome. Focusing on the journey rather than solely on the destination fosters a sense of gratitude and empowerment, which is invaluable during tough times.

By adopting a growth mindset, individuals can transform their approach to failure and setbacks, viewing them as stepping stones to success rather than insurmountable obstacles. This mindset shift is key to personal development and achieving one's full potential.

Channel Negative Emotions into Determination

Being unable to do something you intended can cause anger, despair, or self-doubt. However, growth-minded people know these sentiments are short-lived and can be turned into motivation and resolution. We can overcome bad feelings without letting them stop us. Problems might help us achieve our goals by turning anger and despair into resolve and determination. After each setback, we are more determined to overcome obstacles and achieve our goals. In pursuit of our dreams, we will constantly make mistakes and fail; with a growth mindset, we may use these challenges to learn and grow. View setbacks as learning opportunities, failing as chances to grow, and use negative emotions as motivation to empower ourselves to overcome obstacles. We can overcome any challenge if we're committed, persistent, and trust in our abilities to learn and improve.

Tracking and Celebrating Progress

Success tracking keeps us motivated and on track as we work toward our goals. We'll discuss techniques to celebrate modest accomplishments and stay inspired to work toward growth mindset goals.

Goal Tracking Apps to Record Progress

In our digital age, goal-tracking applications like Strides, Goals OnTrack, Trello, Lattice, etc., are vital for achieving goals. These applications make it easier to measure progress, stay organized, and focus on long-term goals. They help people track their progress and manage their growth mindset goals.

Trello:

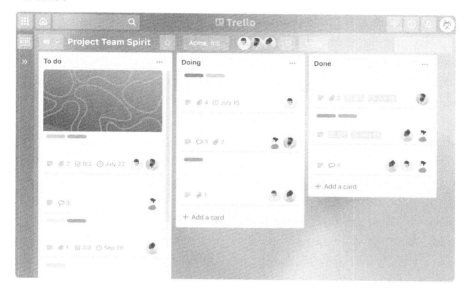

Goals On Track:

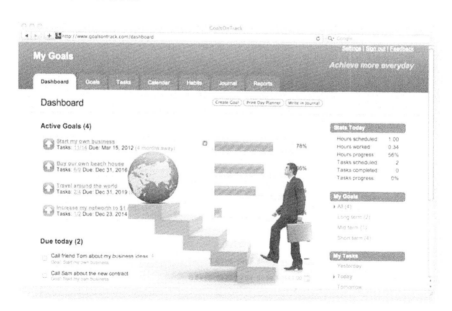

They make it easier to develop SMART goals - specific, measurable, achievable, realistic, and time-bound. Users may measure their progress with defined goals and verifiable targets as clarity illuminates their path and motivates and holds them accountable.

Registering and updating status lets users track their modest wins and identify areas for improvement. This feedback loop keeps users focused on their goals and helps them make smart performance-enhancing choices.

Notifications and notes are another useful feature of goal-tracking apps. Alerts can help users recall tasks and stick to their goals. These alerts help you remain on track and minimize procrastination, whether it's a daily reminder to practice a new skill or a weekly check-in.

Dashboards, charts, and graphs in goal-tracking apps show users their progress; these graphics make trends, patterns, and performance easy to track. Many goal-tracking apps also allow sharing and collaboration, so sharing goals with friends, family, and coworkers holds users accountable and garners support. This social aspect fosters community and motivates individuals to support and appreciate each other.

SMART Goals

SPECIFIC Straightforward, precise and easily defined	MEASURABLE Easy to measure the progress and performance	ARCHIEVABLE The goal is important and possible.	REALISTIC The goals are realistic and relevant.	TIME-BOUND It has a timeline, and a deadline set
Launch 5 new products online and 4 on stores.	To get 5 new products we need to do 5 proposals, 10 pitches and 10 prospects	On average, last quarterly we got 3 new products, and worked on another one	Normally our new products get a special place on our site	Until the end of the quarterly
Increase selling numbers by 10% of not best selling products by increasing user flow	User testing and study of web flow, prior, during and after.	We well learn more about the user wich will help in the creation of new products	We will make changes on the site to make it more useful for the user	Until the end of the quarterly
Implement new time routines for the team adding more evaluation time	Adding meeting times in the teams schedule where we discuss evaluation of products	It will me a meeting of 30 mins where the team discusses	That time will be implemented to create better products	Until the end of the quarterly

Monthly Self-Assessments of Growth

Conducting monthly self-evaluations is a powerful tool for fostering a growth mindset. They serve as a structured way for individuals to reflect on their progress and set clear objectives for personal development. Here's how they can be beneficial:

- **Recognizing Achievements:** By reflecting on their progress toward goals, individuals can feel proud of what they've accomplished. This sense of achievement not only boosts happiness but also serves as a strong motivator for continued growth and learning.

- **Identifying Challenges:** Monthly self-evaluations help pinpoint current challenges or areas of concern. Acknowledging these issues enables individuals to understand their impact on others and themselves, facilitating the search for effective solutions.

- **Highlighting Areas for Improvement:** Through self-reflection, individuals can identify specific areas where more effort is needed. Self-awareness is crucial for achieving various objectives, whether it's acquiring new skills, modifying negative behaviors, or overcoming limiting beliefs.

- **Adjusting Strategies for Growth:** Based on insights gained from self-reflection, individuals can fine-tune their strategies for personal development. This might involve revising action plans, seeking additional support, or experimenting with new approaches to overcome obstacles.

- **Promoting Accountability:** Regular self-evaluations encourage a sense of personal accountability for one's own growth and successes. People who take responsibility for their development are more likely to persevere in their efforts and take decisive action toward their goals.

- **Facilitating Self-Discovery:** Self-evaluation is also an opportunity for self-discovery. Reflecting on past experiences and personal tendencies helps individuals gain a deeper understanding of themselves, unlocking their potential for personal and professional growth.

In essence, monthly self-evaluations are a valuable practice for anyone aiming to cultivate a growth mindset. They enable continuous personal development through structured reflection and strategic action.

Ask yourself these questions given in the box below during monthly self-assessments:

By evaluating yourself regularly, you can stay aware of your progress, celebrate your wins, and find ways to grow and improve.

Self-Assessment Questions

1. How far along am I with my goals for this month?
2. What problems did I face, and how did I solve them?
3. What new skills or ideas have I picked up?
4. How can I change my plans for the future so that I can keep making progress?

Fun Rewards that Reinforce Growth Mindset

Celebrate accomplishments and recognize minor wins to maintain a growth mindset. Shifting focus from the end outcomes to the journey and work done along the way can motivate and inspire people to improve. Success motivates and engages growth-seekers. It boosts their self-esteem, making them more willing to persevere when things go tough. Rewarding minor successes reinforces the concept that skills can be enhanced through commitment and hard work, making people more motivated to take on challenges and perceive losses as opportunities to learn.

Movie nights with friends, special meals at your favorite restaurants, or spa days are unique ways to reward yourself for improvement. Hiking to scenic vistas, attempting new outdoor activities, or visiting nearby cities might all help you unwind. Investing in classes, workshops, seminars, or new interests supports the idea that learning is lifelong. People are happier and more committed to personal and professional improvement when they receive personalized rewards like new books, home spa days, or time with loved ones.

Fun activities make the growth mindset journey more rewarding and motivate people to learn and improve. Celebrating successes and little wins reminds people of their abilities and motivates them to learn and grow. Some fun rewards that can help build a growth mindset are:

- Participating in a favorite sport or activity for yourself.
- Spending time with family or friends.
- Taking care of yourself by doing things like yoga or mindfulness.
- Making time to read a book or watch a movie.

By adding fun rewards to the journey toward our goals, we can maintain a positive attitude and enjoy the process of growth and development. Tracking and appreciating our progress keeps us motivated and on pace to attain our goals. Goal-tracking applications, monthly self-evaluations, and enjoyable prizes that promote a growth mindset help people measure their progress, relish their triumphs, and stay motivated. You can succeed if you work hard, persevere, and grow.

Key Takeaways

- View abilities as flexibility to grow, not as fixed traits.
- Focus on effort and progress rather than perfect outcomes.
- Reframe failures and setbacks as learning opportunities.
- Be patient with the process; growth takes time.

Summary Action Plan

- Set growth mindset goals.
- Choose one to two goals you'd like to accomplish this year.
- Assess what skills or knowledge these goals require and any potential obstacles.
- Break down goals into milestones, focusing on concrete progress and effort.

You can use the following table to sort out your thoughts.

GOAL 1	GOAL 2

GOAL 1		GOAL 2	
SKILLS	OBSTACLES	SKILLS	OBSTACLES

WEEKLY MILESTONES
WEEK 1
WEEK 2
WEEK 3
WEEK 4

CHAPTER 4

Growth Environment

"We do not think ourselves into new ways of living. We live ourselves into new ways of thinking."

-Richard Rohr

APPLYING A GROWTH mentality in relationships can strengthen bonds. This chapter shares tips for improving your social skills, handling conflict better, and developing emotional intelligence to kick-start your journey toward professional growth.

Growth Mindset in Friendships

Having meaningful friendships is vital to our well-being and happiness, but many individuals struggle to develop and maintain them. A growth mindset stresses that social abilities can be learned through practice, which can transform friendships. This approach encourages introverts and shy people to embrace their traits and seek growth through new social contacts.

Belief in the Expandability of Social Skills

The growth mentality for friendships is important. You must understand that social skills can be learned and improved with practice, eventually impacting our networking skills. Social interactions can be improved by practice, like a hobby or skill. Only by accepting this fact can people improve their social abilities independently. Social skills training, such as communication and empathy, has been found to improve relationships, as found by psychological research (Riggio, 2013). This proves the importance of a growth mindset by showing that this area of life may improve.

Viewing Introversion and Shyness as Developable Traits

Shy or introverted people may feel out of place in a socially active society. However, a growth mindset sees shyness and introversion as learnable attributes.

Introversion, or wanting to think alone, can help you connect. Listening and one-on-one conversations help introverts build relationships (Cain, 2013). If they practice their talents, introverts can have fulfilling social lives while being themselves.

Fact Check

Having good friends can even help you live longer. Friendships make you healthier and happier and protect you from some diseases and early death. One study found that having just three close friends or family members can reduce your risk of dying by almost 50%.

Hard work and exposure can overcome shyness, which can make socializing uncomfortable. Exposure to more social interactions and learning to manage discomfort can help people leave their comfort zones and become more socially comfortable (Carducci, 2009). Thinking shyness may be improved, which gives people the strength to face social challenges.

Seeking Growth Through New Social Connections

A development mentality in friendships sees new relationships as opportunities to learn and improve. People with a growth mentality do not find socializing scary or hard. Instead, they see it as an opportunity to learn and socialize.

You must leave your comfort zone and admit your weaknesses to create new opportunities. Some examples are starting conversations with strangers, joining clubs or social groups, or attending events with like-minded people. Although these responsibilities may appear challenging initially, every contact is an opportunity to learn and grow.

Maintaining an open mind and learning from others helps you build genuine connections. Everyone we encounter has a distinct story and perspective. Open, compassionate talks help us understand the world and connect with others.

Practical Strategies for Cultivating a Growth Mindset in Friendships

1. **Set achievable goals:** Write down social skills or areas for improvement and set achievable goals. Breaking down larger tasks into smaller, more achievable steps can help you start a conversation, listen closely, or show empathy.
2. **Make active listening a habit:** Listen to others while they speak. Instead of responding, attempt to comprehend their feelings. Active listening improves connections and displays respect and understanding.
3. **Embrace discomfort:** Know that discomfort frequently leads to growth. Go to a networking event or talk to a stranger to test your knowledge of people. Every experience helps you improve.
4. **Reflect on your past:** Consider the people and things you have done. What worked for you? What could have been improved?

Analyzing past interactions helps you understand yourself and develop new skills.

5. **Request input:** To improve your social skills, consider seeking feedback from friends or professors. Constructive feedback can provide valuable insights.

Be proactive and growth-oriented to create enduring friendships. People can overcome shyness and introversion by believing they can enhance their social abilities with hard work and practice. They can then actively seek new links to grow. Being uncomfortable, setting realistic goals, and practicing active listening can help you grow and deepen your relationships. Approaching friendships with a growth mindset helps people attain their maximum social connection and happiness potential.

Communicating with Empathy

Working communication builds relationships, understanding, and empathy and conveys information. To communicate with empathy, you must actively listen, ask intelligent questions, and affirm others' feelings. These talents can improve over time to help people trust and connect.

Active Listening Without Judgment

Understanding conversation requires active listening, which involves not judging or interrupting. Active listening requires hearing, understanding, and understanding the speaker's intent. Repeating or summarizing what someone said shows you are listening and helps everyone understand. Restating what the other person said in your language shows you understand and value their perspective.

Ask Thoughtful Follow-Up Questions

Effective communication requires more than listening. Engage with what the other person is saying. Asking insightful follow-up questions can help you understand, inspire more study, and demonstrate your genuine interest in the speaker's perspective.

Make follow-up inquiries open-ended and nonjudgmental, so the person can speak more about their feelings and views. Avoid nasty, invasive questions; instead, ask questions that generate thought and emotion. Instead of "Why did you do that?" ask, "Can you tell me more about what led you to make that decision?" This strategy helps both sides comprehend and care about each other by making the speaker think more thoroughly about their motives for speaking.

Validate Others' Emotions to Build Trust

Validating the emotions of others builds trust and empathy. While you may disagree with someone's views or experiences, it is important to validate their feelings. Listen to what someone says and watch for nonverbal signs to support their feelings. Respond with empathy, validating their sentiments without criticizing or judging. When someone says they are going through a hard time, say, "It sounds like you are really overwhelmed right now." Allow them to show their feelings and acknowledge and support their feelings.

Developing Listening, Understanding, and Vulnerability

Learning to comprehend, be vulnerable, and listen requires time and effort. Practice and self-reflection are essential to success; continue to develop your empathy-based communication by trying these:

1. **Be self-aware:** Assess your speaking habits and find ways to improve. Watch your reactions to others' sentiments and talk to them with empathy.
2. **Practice empathy:** Look for ways to exhibit empathy with friends, family, coworkers, and even strangers. Listen, ask

intelligent questions, and acknowledge feelings to connect and understand others.

3. **Seek advice:** Ask trusted individuals about your communication abilities, specifically how well you demonstrate empathy, listen intently, and validate others. Accept constructive criticism and use it to improve.

4. **Reflect on your successes and failures:** Consider your communication successes and failures. Think about how the strategies that helped you comprehend and connect with others and those strategies that did not. Use your newfound knowledge to guide your actions.

> **Rest Time!**
> You must have tried continuous reading. Do the suggested exercise and then continue reading after that:
> Lie down and get lost in your book with these leg lifts.
> Begin with lying down on your right side with your arm propped up for head support.
> Grab your book of choice so that it is nearby for you to read. Lift your leg up and down, and repeat this motion 10 times or read 2 pages before alternating sides

Working on your communication skills, empathy, vulnerability, and active listening can help you build trust and meaningful relationships. As these abilities become more natural and easier to utilize, your personal and corporate interactions will improve.

Overcoming Rejection and Conflict

Creating and maintaining connections always presents challenges, and rejection and conflicts can be upsetting. Seeing relationship losses as opportunities to learn and grow can help people become more resilient and handle interpersonal issues. A growth mindset can help people deal with rejection and disagreement by seeing them as chances to progress personally and in relationships.

Reframing Rejection as an Opportunity for

Understanding

Rejection is familiar, yet it can leave you feeling let down, inadequate, and self-conscious. However, rejection can teach people valuable lessons if they use it to identify what went wrong. Rejection can help people understand themselves and progress instead of making them feel worthless or unable. People can learn about themselves and their relationships by examining what happened before and after the rejection and what they could have done differently.

If a romantic relationship ends, someone can reflect on their communication, emotional availability, and compatibility. Knowing what they must improve can help them approach future conversations with self-awareness and purpose.

See Conflicts as Chances to Improve Dispute Resolution Skills

Disputes are inevitable, whether with a partner, friend, family member, or workplace. While they can hurt, arguments can also improve problem-solving and strengthen relationships. Instead of avoiding or worsening confrontations, people might view them as opportunities to understand one another and find a solution. Positive interactions, empathy, and problem-solving can turn arguments into opportunities for growth and peace. To resolve disputes, people must communicate well, understand others, and work together to create a solution that works for everyone.

Use Emotional Self-Regulation Tactics Until Able to Discuss Issue Calmly

Discussions often involve emotions, making it difficult to reach solutions. Emotional self-regulation aids in problem-solving and managing emotions.

This approach helps to reduce emotions and bring clarity, improving communication and problem-solving. Speaking correctly lets people state their wants and needs with strength and respect. "I" statements, active listening, and empathy help people resolve conflicts and maintain relationships.

Strong, self-aware, and willing to learn and grow are needed to overcome rejection and disagreement. Change your mindset and use growth concepts like understanding, conflict resolution, and emotional self-regulation to turn relationship issues into growth opportunities. This can help them develop personally and romantically and build deeper, longer-lasting relationships built on confidence, respect, and understanding.

Role Playing Challenging Situations

Communication skills are critical in any relationship, but they improve with practice as no one is perfect from the start; everyone requires experiences, both good and bad, to learn from them and improve communications. Through challenges in the relationship, people tend to experience many things along the way, which helps them to learn through ideas gathered during the challenging circumstances they are facing. There are a few rejections that not only tear apart the heart of a person but also have a severe impact on overall life decisions.

These rejections are discussed below, along with their solutions, so that you can get through those challenges quickly. They are how to handle a crush's rejection, a disagreement with parents, and getting back together with friends after a conflict. The role-playing activities suggested in this reading passage will help you practice growth mindset communication, which will be helpful in the long run.

Handling Rejection from a Crush

Facing rejection from the person you love the most is seriously a challenging situation to be in, and it is tremendously hard to get out of that situation. Only the person who went through it can understand what it feels like. However, along with a challenge, it also presents an opportunity to improve yourself and give yourself enough time to self-reflect your personality and improve it for the next person in your life. For self-reflection, you first have to imagine a situation in your mind where you have been rejected by the person you loved so much and have faced a harsh rejection from that person. After that, you should follow the role-playing exercises mentioned below:

Role-playing Exercise:

1. Think like a person telling their crush how they feel.
2. Practice speaking clearly and honestly, expressing your feelings while respecting the other person's space.
3. Listen carefully when playing the crush. Show empathy and acknowledge the other person's bravery in expressing themselves.
4. Switch roles and rehearse again so everyone can see both sides.

Key Communication Skills to Practice:

- Expressing emotions assertively and respectfully
- Active listening and empathy
- Accepting rejection gracefully and maintaining dignity

Resolving an Argument with Parents

As we grow, we have different perspectives as we are exposed to different atmospheres and people from different races. Due to those differences, you tend to make other and unique career choices and compete with your colleagues, so argument with your parents is natural. Here are some of the role-playing exercises you can do to neutralize the conflicts with your parents:

Role-playing Exercise:

Imagine yourself as a child and share your concerns and wishes for their future. Act like a kid to practice active listening and empathy. Support your parents' concerns while expressing yourself. Work together to find compromises that satisfy both sides. Switch roles and rehearse again so that everyone can see both sides.

Key Communication Skills to Practice:

- Active listening and empathy
- Expressing thoughts and feelings assertively and respectfully
- Collaborative problem-solving and compromise

Reconnecting after a Conflict with Friends

You must have seen in movies and your personal life that a circle of friends who have been together forever suddenly have a conflict, and the friendship suffers.

This can happen if one does not resolve the conflict immediately by taking the necessary measures. For example, if you recently had a disagreement with your friend, initiate the conversation yourself and try to rebuild your connection with him. Follow the role-playing exercise for reconnecting with your friends after a conflict:

Role-playing Exercise:

1. To reconnect, be the friend who starts the conversation. Say you want to discuss the issue and work towards repairing the friendship.
2. Take turns acknowledging each other's thoughts and perspectives and trying to understand rather than blame.
3. Together, come up with steps to solve the problem and restore trust, such as saying sorry, setting limits, or promising to talk to each other more often.
4. Change roles and practice again so everyone can see both sides.

Key Communication Skills to Practice:

- Initiating difficult conversations with empathy and sincerity
- Active listening and validating others' emotions
- Collaborative problem-solving and commitment to resolution

Role-playing challenging relationship scenarios helps people practice speaking skills in a safe and supportive environment. Growth mindset ideas like empathy, active listening, and problem-solving help people navigate difficult situations. Regular practice and reflection can enhance and use these real-life skills, fostering understanding, connection, and resilience.

If you want to live a life entirely of learning and growing, adopt the ideas of a growth mindset. Commit to learning new things throughout your life, encourage self-reflection, build resilience, and make friends who can help you. Take advantage of every chance to learn and grow and remember that failures are just steps to success. Accept that failing is a normal part of the journey and use it to fuel your drive to keep going. Every step you take will bring you one step closer to reaching your full potential and having a meaningful life. Start your trip today and discover all the amazing things waiting for you.

Key Takeaways

- Social skills can be developed over time through effort.
- Setbacks in relationships provide learning opportunities.
- Feedback from others helps us identify areas for growth.
- Empathy, vulnerability, and listening are skills to build.
- Progress takes patience; change thinking and habits first.

Summary Action Steps: Set Relationship Growth Goals

- Choose 1-2 relationship areas to focus growth efforts on over the next few months.
- Identify current challenges and select skills to develop, such as communication, perspective-taking, emotion regulation, and conflict management.
- Break goals down into measurable steps.
- Seek input from trusted friends and mentors.

Activities:

Relationship Growth Goals	Activity 1
Personal Reflection: Write down 1 to 2 relationship areas you want to focus on and why.	

Relationship Growth Goals	Activity 2
Identify Challenges: List specific challenges you face in these relationship areas.	

Relationship Growth Goals	Activity 3
Select Skills to Build: Choose skills you want to develop to address these challenges.	

Relationship Growth Goals	Activity 4
Action Steps: Break your goals down into measurable steps you can take.	

CHAPTER 5

Growing into Your Best Self

"It's not that I'm so smart, it's just that I stay with problems longer."

-Albert Einstein

THIS CHAPTER DISCUSSES continually developing your best self through identifying areas for growth, cultivating new skills and interests, and maintaining a growth mindset lifestyle.

Identifying Areas for Growth

Understanding Myself: Personality Tests

Tests like the Myers-Briggs Type Indicator (MBTI) and Big Five personality traits will reflect your introverted or extroverted, intuitive or sensing, thinking or feeling, and determining or perceiving personalities. These are going to reveal your thinking, feeling, and acting inclinations, explaining your reactions in diverse situations.

Personality assessments reveal your strengths and skills; for example, an extroverted person may excel in social roles, whereas an introverted person may excel in skills that can be performed alone without anyone's interruption. Knowing and using your talents will help you succeed at work and home and be happier.

The tests reveal your flaws and areas that need improvement. Perfectionists may need help with delegation and time management, and a less focused person may need more structure and discipline. Knowing your weaknesses does help, as you can then improve on those weaknesses and become a better person. For that, you can find a mentor or attend training and development programs.

Assessing Skills: SWOT Analysis

Understanding your strengths is key to unlocking your true potential; these are the areas where you are extremely good, such as technical, communication, leadership, or artistic talents. Recognizing and harnessing these capabilities can propel you toward your goals and aspirations.

However, your weaknesses show where you can progress. You may feel insecure, lack abilities, or know too little about yourself, but knowing those weaknesses allows you to fix them through training, coaching, or focused practice.

Looking at opportunities also helps you uncover outside influences that could help you flourish. These may be new trends, opportunities to meet new people, or environmental changes that help you advance in your career. By seizing these opportunities, you may extend your perspectives and maximize excellent situations.

> **Tip**
> Get feedback from your close friend or family member about your growth and reflect on that feedback on what you need to improve to make yourself better for the future.

Threats help you prepare for problems you may face. These include dire economic circumstances, technical advances, and peer or foe competition. Awareness of these concerns allows you to reduce risks and plan for potential issues.

Defining Values: Shaping Life Purpose Goals

- Activities that assist you in identifying your values are crucial to finding your life purpose. Your principles guide you to happiness and purpose in life and work.
- Self-discovery begins with these exercises: When you examine your core values and their meaning, your values — honesty, inventiveness, kindness, and toughness — guide your decisions and actions.
- Finding your basic principles ensures that your ambitions match your most profound wants. Aiming for personal fulfillment and values-aligned goals makes your efforts more meaningful.
- If family is essential to you, you will prioritize work-life balance and hunt for positions that allow you to spend more time with them.
- This connection delights you because your work matters. Your work is meaningful because it contributes to something greater.
- Living the values also strengthens you when you confront challenges. Your principles strengthen in difficult times. They keep you grounded in what matters and offer strength, which is extremely useful.

Assessing Yourself: Understanding Skills, Values, and Interests

Finding your skills, values, and interests helps you focus on your goals and overall happiness.

Thinking about the past and what others have said about you helps to identify your strengths and weaknesses. This honest review helps to focus your growing efforts. Discovering your essential values — honesty, creativity, society, or anything else — helps you grasp the information and details of what matters the most. These principles guide you toward authentic objectives and activities that give significance to life.

You approach your interests with curiosity and openness, seeking numerous opportunities to learn and grow. You are open to working on new opportunities that make you happy and inspire your interests, whether it is a new pastime, school, or community service. Knowing your strengths, limitations, values, and hobbies helps you make good job and personal growth decisions. Now that you know yourself better, you can design a meaningful, rewarding, and authentic path for advancement.

Determining Goals for Self-Improvement

Now that you know me better and have considered my skills, values, and hobbies, you will be setting clear, achievable self-improvement goals. To achieve some of these goals, you may need to gain new skills or improve in a field related to your interests and ambitions. You might want to learn a new programming language, improve a foreign language, or study a job — or interest-related topic.

Other goals include developing values-based and health-promoting practices. These could entail starting a regular exercise program, meditating, practicing mindfulness, or prioritizing self-care like sleep and work-life balance. Every goal has specific milestones, due dates, and measurements. Dividing larger ambitions into smaller, more achievable tasks keeps you going and progressing.

I'm also open to adjusting my plans as you work toward your goals because growth is ongoing. You can use setbacks to learn and improve and stay strong and driven. Setting specific, achievable self-improvement goals empowers you to lead your evolution.

As Buddha said, "What we think, we become."

Embracing the Journey

As you begin your self-improvement path, you should look forward to challenges and opportunities. You should understand that progress is not always linear, and mistakes may happen, but you still aim to achieve your potential and lead a meaningful and fulfilling life. You should be grateful for every stride, big or small, and tackle issues with determination. You gain strength and motivation from the journey as you uncover new parts of yourself and unlock possibilities.

Cultivating New Skills and Interests

As you learn new talents and activities, you will be excited to challenge yourself and progress even further.

Embracing Public Speaking Training

If you want to learn a new skill and challenge yourself to step out of your comfort zone, public speaking lessons can be very helpful. Even if the idea of speaking in front of a crowd makes you uneasy, you probably know how important it is to practice. Joining a public speaking club or taking classes can provide you with a safe and supportive space to practice this skill.

You should be seeing an opportunity to speak — presenting a prepared speech or participating in speaking exercises — as a challenge and push yourself to overcome any fears. Practice makes you more confident in your public speaking skills. You learn to control your anxiety, speak clearly, and hold people's attention with engaging and convincing lectures.

Exploring Dance Classes

Dance classes provide a unique opportunity to master new talents and express yourself. Getting on the dance floor may be intimidating initially, mainly if you need to get used to moving. You should enjoy trying new, creative, and expressive dance class expressions. It enables you to express your feelings, stories, and experiences powerfully and freely. Success requires effort and persistence; you might stumble and fall, but you can tackle obstacles and leave your comfort zone to achieve success.

Dancing Tips:

- Practice regularly to improve your coordination and muscle memory.
- Focus on posture and body alignment to enhance balance and gracefulness.
- Learn to feel the rhythm of the music and adapt your movements accordingly.
- Experiment with different styles of dance to broaden your skillset and creativity.
- Don't be afraid to express yourself and let go of inhibitions while dancing.

Every step, sway, and whirl improves your balance, rhythm, and grace. When you meet other people who are music and movement lovers, you learn more about the art form and culture. Dance classes help you discover hidden talents and expand your abilities. They make you strong, disciplined, and driven to overcome obstacles. Dance helps you uncover and express yourself, showing you that growth isn't simply mental. The body and spirit experience it, too.

Immersing in a Foreign Language Instruction

Learning a new language helps you improve personally. Putting yourself in unique situations speeds up your learning and helps you become fluent faster. Early immersion can be difficult as you learn new words and language structures, but these challenges are opportunities to learn and grow. Every conversation teaches you something new, and you always look for ways to improve your language skills.

Whenever you speak the target language, you feel more secure and proficient. You are more comfortable communicating, understanding, and solving daily problems in the language.

These events strengthened your language abilities and taught you about various cultures.

Immersion programs also allow you to meet other language learners; your community encourages and pushes you to improve, and the group contains native speakers and language learners.

Learning a second language helps you explore yourself and other cultures. You are excited about learning a new language because of its challenges and benefits. Each step pushes you closer to fluency and opens new doors.

Stepping Outside My Comfort Zone

Your growth journey requires you to leave your comfort zone, and you keep repeating to yourself that growth comes from pushing your limits and accepting the anguish of the unknown. Stepping outside your comfort zone improves your talents and comprehension of the world. You learn how to handle new situations, get stronger when things go wrong, and gain confidence in your capacity to overcome obstacles.

You also know that leaving your comfort zone is a continuous process; change and growth bring new challenges. To progress personally and professionally, you must push yourself beyond your limits. You look forward to growing and changing with every step outside your comfort zone, and you like pain because it motivates you to be your best. With each problem, you become stronger, more durable, and more capable.

Remembering Competencies Develop Over Time

As you attempt to enhance your skills, you must realize that your abilities expand over time. Mastery takes time, commitment, and patience. It is easy to fall into the trap of expecting results quickly. You convince yourself that just as Rome was not built in a day, your talents would not improve slowly. Instead, you go into every assignment with a growth mindset, knowing that success is slow and happens repeatedly.

Seeking Growth Opportunities Purposefully

Actively seeking growth opportunities helps you better your abilities and uncover your potential. You consciously choose tools and support systems that aid your development. For example, you can take a course, attend a workshop, or seek mentorship from industry leaders.

You know that growth requires planning and a commitment to learning and growing. You pursue mastery and self-fulfillment by taking charge and grasping growth opportunities. You deliberately seek workshops and courses aligning with your career goals, hobbies, and interests. These opportunities teach you, provide you with skills, and equip you for success in many areas. Apart from that, you value mentoring and seek guidance from professionals in your growth areas. Successful people provide you with ideas and information that accelerate your growth. You welcome the discomfort that frequently comes with growth opportunities because you know you need to step out of your comfort zone. You like the difficulties and unknowns of exploring new places, whether it is dance courses, language immersion programs, public speaking workshops, or other things outside your comfort zone.

You must leave your comfort zone and accept growth challenges to learn new talents and hobbies. By actively seeking growth opportunities, you learn, progress, and discover new possibilities.

Maintaining a Growth Mindset Lifestyle

As you commit to a growth mindset, you must embrace principles and best practices to keep growing and improving. This section will discuss techniques for maintaining this attitude, which will empower you to overcome obstacles, persevere, and improve.

Replacing Fixed Mindset Thoughts with Growth Reflections

To start your life of growth and potential, you shift your fixed mindset thoughts to growth reflections. Instead of regard failures as insurmountable obstacles, you see them as opportunities to learn and grow.

When you are struggling, you consciously avoid negative thinking and view every challenge as a chance to learn and improve. You approach circumstances with curiosity and openness, eager to gain insights and enhance yourself.

You recognize that with hard effort and dedication, you can improve your skills. There is no innate talent or limit for you; you believe you can overcome any obstacle and achieve your goals with drive and tenacity. This mindset shift motivates you to improve continually and gives you the courage to face every challenge. You see failures as stepping stones to achievement rather than setbacks.

Setting Learning-Oriented Goals Each Month

Having monthly learning goals helps you keep on pace for personal growth and improvement. These goals steer you toward new experiences, skills, and knowledge that will improve your happiness and growth.

- Every month, you consider how you want to change. You state your health, hobbies, and professional goals for the month. These goals are about learning and improving, not just achieving results. You aim to learn more and enhance your talents with an open mind.
- You might try to master a new hobby or skill. You work hard to thoroughly immerse yourself in the learning process, whether learning an instrument, photography, or a new artistic medium. You adore discovering and growing.

- You might also set learning goals. You constantly seek new knowledge and perspectives, whether through reading, classes, seminars, or online courses.
- You may also seek to develop abilities for personal or professional growth. Whether it is improving your communication, leadership, or technical skills, you are committed to purposeful practice and skill-building.
- You intentionally progress by setting monthly learning goals. These goals help you see things clearly and encourage you to pursue your dreams. They also excite and engage you, making your journey exciting and new.
- You establish goals to continually learn and improve to create a meaningful, fulfilling existence. Every objective you achieve moves you closer to becoming your best and living a meaningful life.

Allowing Grace Through Gradual Progress Focused on Enjoyment

You understand the importance of enjoying each stage rather than focusing solely on the eventual objective. You celebrate your victories, whether they are learning a new skill, solving an issue, or reaching a broader objective. It makes you feel better about yourself and provides you with a sense of success that motivates you.

Fun while learning is equally important to you; success doesn't define growth for you. You approach everything with an open mind and are eager to learn and experience. You love new things and seek opportunities to learn, grow, and expand. By making your work fun, you create a long-term growth approach that benefits your mind and spirit. Enjoyment and grace availed through modest progress help you see growth more fully. It's about enjoying the journey, finding satisfaction in learning new things, and getting to know yourself better, not merely achieving the peak or a goal. This mindset makes you strong, long-lasting, and content, improving every aspect of your life.

Applying Principles Studied Habitually

You challenge yourself daily to learn from comments. You view feedback as an opportunity to improve rather than condemnation. You're always open to input, whether from others or by reflecting on your performance. Another key to a growth mentality is maintaining a positive attitude when things go wrong. You tackle failures and issues with strength and hope, not despair. Problems teach you how to improve, so you use them. Making these ideals part of your thinking and acting requires consistency. You maintain a growth mindset in your behaviors and actions by being mindful and purposeful. You urge and repeat to create lasting personal improvement.

> *"Attitude is the 'little' thing that makes a big difference."*
>
> **-Winston Churchill**

Continuing Setting Learning-Oriented Goals

Setting learning goals is crucial to your growth mentality. It's about personal growth and ongoing improvement, not just accomplishing goals. Reaching a goal helps you reach higher ones. Instead of being satisfied with your achievements, you utilize them to push yourself to achieve greater perfection in all aspects of your life.

This procedure requires an open mind about the future. You always seek to improve and progress, never settling for the ordinary. You're passionate about any goal, whether learning a new skill, improving, or working on a passion project. You also realize that learning and growth never end. There are always new issues, talents, and viewpoints to explore. Living a lifelong learning mindset ensures that you continually learn, improve, and grow.

You work toward a limitless future by setting learning goals and keeping an open mind. Every objective you achieve is a step toward self-discovery and growth. Every step brings you closer to your potential and a fulfilling life.

Remembering Progress Fluctuates

Remember that change isn't always linear. When everything falls into place, and you're working rapidly, you'll progress tremendously toward your goals. Things sometimes change or go backward, and growth may appear slow or nonexistent.

Kindness and strength are needed in terrible times. Instead of quitting, you can use them to reflect and improve. Seeing these changes as typical elements of the trip helps you maintain your commitment to ongoing improvement.

Accepting these adjustments requires trusting the process. You must believe that things are progressing, albeit slowly or in less evident ways. Every incident, good or bad, has lessons and insights. These help you mature.

Accepting the ups and downs of success is critical to a growth attitude; you keep your promise to improve by handling changes with ease and vigor. You build long-term personal growth and fulfillment by being focused, persistent, and open to learning from victories and losses. You're confident you can learn and discover yourself throughout your lives.

Finding Growth Partnership

Being with like-minded folks helps you grow. This chapter will explain growth partnerships and how to locate and establish them.

Seeking Out Growth-Oriented Peers

Friends who value improvement are like a supporting community, encouraging and guiding you on your personal development journey. These people inspire and motivate you to try new things and succeed.

You often discuss ideas, experiences, and perspectives, which helps you improve. Growth-oriented buddies bring deep insights and learning to conversations.

You seek growth-oriented peers by building honest, shared-values interactions. You prefer people with curiosity, resilience, and a desire to challenge themselves. You share experiences and support one another to push yourselves out of your comfort zones and grow. Hanging out with growth-minded folks is a vow to yourself to grow. They give you support, encouragement, and accountability to work hard for your goals with love and purpose. You change together and push each other to do your best.

Identifying Mentors Aligned with My Goals

Finding mentors who share your goals is like finding guiding lights that provide insight, encouragement, and perspective as you traverse your growth journey. These mentors inspire you with their experiences and expertise to succeed and be happy. Mentors provide wisdom from years of experience, not simply counsel. They have endured the hardships you will face and become wiser and more robust. Their counsel helps you achieve your goals with clarity and purpose. You want mentors who share your beliefs, goals, and future vision, not just those with big resumes or titles. You intentionally seek mentors who share your goals and values of growth, authenticity, and integrity. Their advice isn't just about achievement but about finding contentment and purpose that matches your ideals.

You aggressively seek mentors who may provide valuable ideas and perspectives through structured mentorship programs, networking events, or luck. You treat these connections with humility and respect because you know that learning is a two-way street and that your mentors benefit as much as you do. Your mentors give you insight and constant support. They encourage you to push yourself and do new things even when you doubt yourself. Their advice empowers you to forge your path and learn from success and disappointment.

You develop respectful, trusting, and genuine connections with your mentors. They are more than consultants or role models; they are companions on your path to achieving your goals. They give you direction, bravery, and conviction to follow your dreams with passion and purpose.

Joining Clubs or Online Communities Centered Around Self-Improvement

You enjoy joining self-improvement organizations or online groups to meet new people, form growth partnerships, and develop in a supportive environment.

These online and offline locations unite people who want to grow, learn, and improve. Whether it's a professional group, a neighborhood reading club, or an internet forum, these groups provide many avenues to collaborate. Discussions, collaborative projects, and shared experiences teach you a lot, motivating you to expand your horizons. People can also support each other in these groups. As members grow personally, they can support, advise, and inspire one another.

You can work together to progress and feel supported. By joining these groups or online communities, you can meet more growth-minded people and find mentors with similar beliefs. Through essential contacts, you create a supportive ecosystem in these places, which helps you grow and reach your potential. You take advantage of self-improvement groups and online communities to develop a network of support and inspiration that accelerates your personal growth and makes your life more joyful. These meaningful connections give you information and direction and make you feel like you belong as you grow and be happy.

You have now acquired strategies to broaden your knowledge, nurture your talents, and strive to become the best version of yourself. However, developing a growth mindset has an impact beyond just personal achievement and fulfillment. In the final chapter, we will delve into the tremendous power of growth mindsets to spark positive change across various spheres when embraced collectively in communities, companies, and institutions.

Key Takeaways

- Learning abilities can always be developed
- Stepping outside comfort zones leads to growth
- Progress requires regular effort over time
- Mindsets shape achievement more than innate talents

Take a Quiz!

1. What is one benefit of personality assessments like the Myers-Briggs Type Indicator (MBTI) and the Big Five traits?
   a. They provide fixed labels for individuals.
   b. They limit personal and professional growth.
   c. They reveal strengths, weaknesses, and inclinations.
   d. They have no impact on decision-making.

2. What is a component of a SWOT Analysis?
   a. Key Performance Indicators (KPIs)
   b. Opportunities and Threats
   c. Skills and Interests
   d. Personal Values

3. How can identifying personal values influence career decisions?
   a. It limits career options.
   b. It ensures a mismatch between goals and values.
   c. It helps prioritize work-life balance.
   d. It has no effect on career satisfaction.

4. Why is it important to assess one's skills, values, and interests?
   a. To limit personal growth opportunities.
   b. To make uninformed career decisions.
   c. To plan for personal growth and career development.
   d. To ignore potential areas of improvement.

5. How does embracing a growth mindset affect one's approach to challenges?
   a. It leads to avoidance of challenges.
   b. It encourages giving up easily.
   c. It fosters resilience and determination.
   d. It promotes a fixed mindset.

Answers:

1. C) They reveal strengths, weaknesses, and inclinations.
2. B) Opportunities and threats
3. C) It helps prioritize work-life balance.
4. C) To plan for personal growth and career development.
5. C) It fosters resilience and determination.

Key Takeaways

- Learning abilities can always be developed
- Stepping outside comfort zones leads to growth
- Progress requires regular effort over time
- Mindsets shape achievement more than innate talents

You can use the following table to sort out your thoughts:

Goal Setting for Self-Improvement

Goal Type	Specific Goal	Action Steps	Deadline
Skill development	Learn a new programming language	Register for an online course and set a daily study time.	Four months
Health and wellness	Start a regular exercise program	Choose an activity you enjoy and schedule it three times a week.	Ongoing
Personal growth	Improve Public Speaking skills	Join a local Toastmasters club and attend weekly.	Seven months

Table: Monthly Reflection on Growth Mindset

Month	Challenges Faced	Learnings	Next Steps
For example: July	Difficulty in maintaining an exercise routine.	Learned the importance of flexibility and adjusting goals.	Plan to try new activities to find what motivates you best.

Make a Difference with Your Review
Guiding Teens toward Bold Choices and Brilliant Paths

"I continue to believe that if children are given the necessary tools to succeed,
they will succeed beyond their wildest dreams!" -David Vitter

People who give without expectation live longer, happier lives and make more money.
So, if we've got a shot at that during our time together, darn it, I'm gonna try.

To make that happen, I have a question for you...

Would you help someone you've never met, even if you never got credit for it?

Who is this person, you ask? They are like you — or, at least, like you used to be — less
experienced, wanting to make a difference, and needing help but not sure where to look.

Our Mission? To teach everyone the skills of making bold decisions and discovering new career
paths. That's the driving force behind everything I do. And the only way we can achieve that is
by reaching out to... well, everyone!

This is where you come in. We often judge a book by its cover (and its reviews), right? So, here's
my ask on behalf of a struggling young mind you've never met:

Please help other TEENS by leaving this book a review.

Your **GIFT** costs **NO MONEY** and takes less than 60 seconds to make real, but
it can change a fellow TEENS **LIFE** forever. Your **Review** could help...

...one more small business provides for their community.
...one more entrepreneur supports their family.
...one more employee gets meaningful work.
...one more client transforms their life.
...one more dream comes true.

To get that **'feel good'** feeling and help this person for real, all you have to do is...and
it takes less than 60 seconds...

Leave a Review!

Simply scan the **QR code** below to leave your review:

[https://www.amazon.com/review/review-your-purchases/?asin=BOOKASIN\]

If you feel good about helping a faceless TEEN, you are my kind of person. **WELCOME TO THE
CLUB.** You're one of us.

I'm even more excited to help you learn Python language more easily than you can possibly
imagine. You'll love the lessons I'm about to share in the coming chapters.

THANK YOU from the bottom of my heart. Now, back to our regularly scheduled programming.

 Your biggest fan,

 Emma Davis

73

CHAPTER 6

Why Developing a Growth Mindset Matters

"With a growth mindset, people believe their abilities can be developed. This view creates a love of learning and resilience."

-Carol Dweck.

WHEN COMMUNITIES, BUSINESSES, and institutions collectively embrace growth mindsets, they catalyze transformative change. This section delves into the wide-ranging effects of adopting either a fixed or growth perspective.

Impacts on Achieving Full Potential

Your thoughts heavily influence your life's journey. Imagine a fork in the road with dreams and goals on one side and doubts and constraints on the other. Right now, your thoughts determine your path. Will you embrace change for growth or cling to old beliefs? Your decision will determine your path to success.

Growth Mindsets Empower People to Accomplish Audacious Goals

With a growth attitude, the world presents unlimited opportunities. Imagine having this mindset—seeing problems as learning opportunities and setbacks as steps toward success. In this mindset, lofty objectives are exciting challenges to overcome. Growing resilience is a decisive benefit of a growth mindset; you know that hard work builds skills. Each failure is a lesson and a step forward. Imagine chasing a seemingly unattainable goal that challenges your entire being, taking risks without fear of failure, and believing your efforts will pay off.

Consider the story of Michael Jordan, a legendary basketball player. His success came after many failures and rejections. Despite these failures, he adopted a growth mentality he used each missed shot and defeat to improve his technique and strength. Jordan changed basketball history with his dedication and undying belief in his ability.

Fixed Mindsets Prematurely Stunt Dreams and Ambitions

Look at it this way: You are trapped in a cage of self-imposed constraints, thinking your skills are fixed. In this state, you will realize that the weight of feeling inadequate kills dreams and goals. A stagnant mentality makes you fearful of failing, limiting your potential. Imagine being terrified of failing at your dreams so you don't pursue them.

Sylvia Plath's journey through life and literature is a poignant reminder of how a fixed mindset can dramatically affect one's well-being and output. Her brilliance in poetry was undeniable, yet her struggles with mental health overshadowed it it was overshadowed by her struggles with mental health. Her fear of not meeting her own high standards became a self-fulfilling prophecy, stifling her ability to see beyond her immediate struggles.

Although celebrated for its intensity and emotional depth, Plath's work also serves as a narrative of her battle with her inner demons.

Her literary genius was both fueled and hindered by her mental state, illustrating the complex relationship between creativity and mental health. Her entrenched worldview imprisoned her creativity and killed her prematurely.

Abilities Viewed as Flexible Allow for Expanded Achievement

Think about a paradigm shift from constraint to freedom. It corroborates that abilities may be developed with hard work and dedication, and those with a growth mindset can achieve anything, overcome self-doubt, and use challenges to improve. Instead of fearing failure, you regard it as a necessary step to success. Change your mind swiftly unlocks doors and leads you to heights you never imagined.

Consider J.K. Rowling, who went from a struggling single mother to literary success. A growth mindset can improve your life, like Rowling's. She may have given up on her aspirations after being rejected by many companies and going through personal hardships. Instead, she had a growth mindset and used each rejection to improve. Harry Potter, which has enthralled millions worldwide, was ultimately written by Rowling, and she did this by practicing writing and believing in herself.

Your thoughts are like the strands of a rug, touching every aspect of your existence. Will you embrace change or hold onto rigid beliefs? Your decision will affect your travel and destination. With a growth mindset, big ambitions become achievable, setbacks become opportunities to progress, and restrictions become stepping stones. However, a fixed mindset might prevent you from achieving your goals and trap you in self-doubt and inaction.

Remember that hard work and dedication can improve your skills. A growth mentality opens unlimited possibilities and points you toward a future limited only by your thinking. When faced with an option, choose wisely; your outlook determines who you are and who you can become.

"Once you replace negative thoughts with positive ones, you'll start having positive results."

-Willie Nelson

Ripple Effects on Others

As you learn to interact with others, you discover that your attitude influences everyone in your community. Imagine living where development mindsets are prevalent, and drive and toughness are strengths that unite individuals. This shows how growth mindsets may improve lives and communities.

Growth Mindsets Create Motivated, Resilient Communities

Being around growth-minded individuals who view issues as learning opportunities and temporary hurdles turns motivation into a contagious force within the community, driving progress and ambition for everyone.

Recovery from issues distinguishes growth-minded groups. Remember losing someone in your personal or professional life. Your community comforts you instead of giving up and giving in to hopelessness, and you weather the storm because you know each other is strong and trust in growth.

Consider the residents of a small town destroyed by a natural disaster. Hopelessness threatens the city after the calamity. A resilient spirit emerges from the rubble, propelled by the concept that everyone can rebuild and prosper jointly. This united mindset helps them heal and persevere.

Peer Effects Spread, Elevating Group Capabilities

Imagine the benefits of growth mindsets spreading rapidly in your community. Imagine your friends and family adopting your growth philosophy after seeing how you think. The group's talents improve because everyone is devoted to growth and excellence. People in growth-friendly communities are more likely to collaborate since they can share skills and expertise. Imagine being on a team pursuing a challenging goal. Your friends' support and knowledge keep you from being overwhelmed. Each member's unique abilities and ideas enhance the group's comprehension and creativity.

Consider how an organization's growth-mindedness affects things; when employees believe in learning and developing, fresh ideas and productivity soar. Every employee wants to push the limits and go above and beyond, which fosters innovation and greatness.

Vulnerabilities and Setbacks Shared Openly to Help Others

A group that wants to grow does not regard vulnerability as a weakness. Consider telling someone about your issues and faults and you can listen to them. Being open helps people connect deeper, leading to trusting and understanding connections.

Being honest about your imperfections encourages others to do so also. Attending a support group where individuals share their journeys and listen to others can help. In this secure atmosphere, people feel strong enough to face challenges, giving them the courage to develop and heal.

Consider how honesty can transform things and help people build helpful groups. When people feel safe discussing their fears, they break down walls and develop bridges. Trust and honesty keep friends for life; these relationships can help people through stressful times. Your thoughts impact your path and your group's.

With a growth mentality, you may motivate, support, and encourage others to make positive changes. As growth mindset communities arise, their shared ideals spread, strengthening the group and driving collaboration and innovation. Toughness empowers a group, and failures are opportunities to flourish.

As you work with challenging individuals, remember that a growth mindset can improve your life and those around you. Encouragement of growth and opportunity creates a better future where people are driven, strong, and can obtain support.

Growth Mindset at Work, Home and Beyond

After applying a development mindset to numerous aspects of your life, it affects more than just you.

Fosters Cultures of Creativity, Collaboration and Innovation

Creativity is unrestrained in a growth mindset company, and teamwork is blooming like never before. Imagine entering this vibrant area where new ideas and possibilities flood every corner. This society values potential, which nurtures innovation like wildflowers in a fertile garden; employees are encouraged and assigned to think creatively, question the current quo, and go where this is the first time anyone has gone. Working for a company that embraces and nurtures all ideas, no matter how odd, makes employees happy and productive.

Collaboration is natural in this growth-oriented environment, and team members' diverse perspectives and wisdom are easily integrated. Imagine working in a group where everyone can speak up and solve complex problems to advance innovation. People cherish differences here because they believe diversity fosters fresh ideas and growth.

Consider how this approach could affect an organization's results. A growth mentality empowers people to innovate and push the limits. The company becomes a hub of inspiration and innovation, where groundbreaking ideas bloom and advance the organization.

A creative, collaborative, and innovative culture influences more than just the company. A successful company draws top personnel driven by its fast-paced culture eager to contribute their skills, ideas, growth, and ingenuity to fuel the success cycle. Using growth mindsets to promote creativity, teamwork,

Poll Result

About 75% of employers rate teamwork and collaboration as "very important," yet only 18% of employees get communication evaluations at their performance reviews.

and innovation can make an organization successful and spark huge improvements. With a growth mindset, people and businesses may maximize their potential, inspire new ideas, and push the envelope for a better, more affluent future.

Employees Become More Engaged, Productive, and Fulfilled

When you think about how growth mindsets affect employee engagement, productivity, and happiness, you imagine a workplace where everyone produces their best job, driven by a shared purpose and continual improvement. Imagine joining an energetic workforce where every day offers fresh opportunities to learn, grow, and be happy.

In this environment, labor is a source of energy and meaning. Employees are empowered and driven to attain their most significant potential when valued and respected. Imagine enthusiastically arriving at work every day, ready to tackle new responsibilities and make a difference.

A growth mindset makes work exciting and hopeful, viewing obstacles as opportunities to learn and improve. Every obstacle is an opportunity to learn and improve and be more motivated to tackle challenging work or endeavor. Instead of fearing failure, you regard it as a necessary step toward success, understanding that every setback teaches you something.

Engaged workers are more productive, driven, and concerned about shared goals. They exceed expectations and use their expertise to create fresh ideas and achieve remarkable achievements. This makes the company more efficient, productive, and profitable, preparing it for long-term success in a fast-changing market.

In addition to company success, a growth-minded workforce enhances employee health and happiness. Employees feel fulfilled and purposeful when they realize they are part of something bigger and that their work matters. This produces a positive workplace where everyone feels respected, supported, and equipped to succeed. A growth mentality significantly impacts employee engagement, productivity, and happiness. Firms foster growth and development to equip employees to attain their most significant potential. This creates success and fresh ideas that improve everyone's future.

Conflict and Differences Viewed as Learning Opportunities

Growth-minded people see conflict and diversity as necessary for progress and new ideas. When entering a meeting room with diverse opinions, each contributing to the conversation, people here are interested and want to understand instead of being defensive or avoiding confrontations.

You have an open mind and learn from peers with various opinions during fruitful talks. You view dispute as an essential element of the creative process, not a sign of failure or dysfunction. Every debate allows one to question beliefs, consider fresh perspectives, and explore new choices; with a growth mindset, you grasp how varied perspectives stimulate new ideas and creativity. Instead of compromising, you must actively seek new perspectives and welcome disagreements since they lead to breakthroughs and new ideas.

Teams that view dispute as a constructive factor are stronger and more flexible. They can better handle the demands of a rapidly changing environment. People accept and even encourage differences because everyone has unique strengths and perspectives. The setting encourages creativity by allowing people to question the established status quo. Team members can collaborate better when they use their distinct skills and perspectives to solve complex problems and propose new ideas.

Seeing disagreements and conflicts as learning opportunities fosters ongoing growth and improvement. Teams become more agile and responsive, making adapting and seizing new opportunities easier. Knowing their work is recognized and that they can learn and grow daily makes people happier and more engaged.

Influencing Organizations and Institutions

As you move through institutions and organizations, you witness how growth mindsets may affect how we work, learn, and run governments. Consider yourself a change agent who encourages growth-oriented practices that foster inventiveness, resilience, and new ideas. You will learn how growth mindsets may assist businesses, schools, the government, and other organizations and how kids like you can help their communities.

Volunteer to Educate on Growth Mindsets

Imagine a workplace where "growth mindsets" are not just a buzzword but a shared ideal. Workers are encouraged to work hard, take measured chances, and learn from failure. You want to help by proposing that your coworkers join training programs that will boost their self-confidence. You envisage classes and seminars that teach workers to cultivate a growth-oriented attitude to attain their full potential and succeed at work.

Growth mindsets help workers solve challenges, adapt to change, and be more creative. They now view failures as opportunities to learn and grow, which improves their performance and productivity.

A company's growth and development attitude boosts employee engagement, happiness, and loyalty. Employees who realize the organization values their growth and well-being feel appreciated and encouraged. This creates a positive feedback loop where enthusiastic employees boost company success. Encouragement of growth mindsets is crucial.

Ultimately, encouraging a growth mindset, education, and empowerment helps shape company culture and ensure long-term success in a competitive market. Your work helps the company, and your teammates grow personally and professionally, fostering success for all.

Thinking about how growth views affect schools opens vital ways to improve things. In a growth mindset classroom, pupils grasp the content and develop the life skills they need after school. When you create growth mindset training sessions at your school, these courses could include workshops and lectures to teach students about the growth mindset and provide them with tools to overcome obstacles, keep going, and see failures as opportunities to learn and improve. These programs will positively affect students' health and academic performance. Students with a growth mindset are more hopeful and can handle scholastic problems. Those who believe hard work will enhance their abilities and improve their success rate are more likely to tackle and finish challenging undertakings. Growing-minded students are more engaged in learning and seek ways to develop their abilities and knowledge; they do not mind taking risks or making errors because they realize these things are vital for their development.

Students work harder and are more determined to solve challenges, which improves their academic performance. By understanding their skills and potential, they also build self-confidence and self-efficacy outside of school. Beyond academic accomplishment, growth mindset training improves students' health and well-being. Schools promote resilience and growth by promoting a safe learning

Fact Check:
86% of employees and executives cite a lack of collaboration or ineffective communication as a cause of workplace failures.

environment, which offers students the courage and hope to face life's challenges.

Start Petitions for Growth Mindset Curriculum

Envisioning the impact of growth mindsets on government agencies and institutions reveals a powerful potential for positive change at the societal level. As you step into advocacy, you see yourself playing a pivotal role in driving this transformative shift by advocating for integrating growth mindset principles into public policies and programs.

Start petitions to implement a growth mindset curriculum in schools and government training programs, rallying support from your peers and community members to effect change. These petitions would highlight the importance of fostering resilience, adaptability, and innovation in the face of complex challenges, emphasizing the need for a paradigm shift in how we approach education and governance.

The transformative potential of such advocacy efforts on societal outcomes is that when government agencies embrace growth mindsets, they become more agile, responsive, and effective in addressing the needs of their constituents. By fostering a culture of experimentation and learning, they are better equipped to tackle pressing issues and navigate the complexities of a rapidly changing world. Moreover, integrating growth mindset principles into public policies and programs has far-reaching implications for communities and individuals. When individuals are empowered to embrace growth mindsets, they become more resilient in the face of adversity, more adaptable to change, and more innovative in their approaches to problem-solving.

As a result, communities thrive, and individuals are empowered to reach their full potential, driving social and economic progress for all. By advocating for integrating growth mindset principles into public policies and programs, you play a vital role in shaping the future of governance and education, ensuring that society is equipped to thrive in an ever-changing world.

By starting petitions for implementing the growth mindset curriculum and advocating for integrating growth mindset principles into public policies and programs, you create a society where resilience, adaptability, and innovation are valued and cultivated at every level. Your efforts pave the way for a brighter future, empowering individuals and communities to overcome challenges and reach their full potential.

Actionable Steps for Teen Readers

Here are some ways teen readers can make a difference in their community:

1. Teach your peers about a development mindset through workshops, seminars, and programs where you mentor students.
2. Promote a growth mindset curriculum in your school by describing how it will make kids more resilient, flexible, and creative learners.
3. Encourage your organization to teach its employees about the growth mindset, emphasizing its importance for personal and business success.
4. Begin campaigns and petitions to persuade peers, community members, and politicians to adopt growth mindset policies and programmers.

Adopting proactive steps can have a transformative impact on your neighborhood. You have the power to promote growth-oriented approaches that enable people and organizations to thrive in a constantly changing world. Let's discuss your strategies for expanding your knowledge, cultivating your talents, and becoming the best version of yourself. With a growth mindset, positive change can be achieved in the world.

Key Takeaways

- Inspires others to realize their full potential
- Develops habits of lifelong learning
- Creates motivated, resilient mindsets
- Provides a foundation for continuous improvement

Action Plan Table:

Step	Action Item	Description	Tools Needed	Target Audience	Timeline
1	Select Participants	Choose three people who would benefit from learning about a growth mindset.	None	Family, friends, colleagues	1 week
2	Prepare Materials	Gather research articles, illustrations, and examples that explain the growth mindset.	Research articles, books, visual aids (diagrams)	-	2 weeks
3	Schedule Sessions	Arrange a convenient time for a discussion or workshop with each person.	Calendar, communication tools (phone, email)	-	3 weeks
4	Conduct Educational Sessions	Break down the core concepts of the growth mindset and show research findings and illustrations.	Prepared materials and presentation tools (PowerPoint)	-	4-6 weeks

5	Follow-Up	Check in with each person to discuss their understanding and implementation of these concepts.	Communication tools, feedback form	-	8 weeks
6	Encourage Continuation of Learning	Provide additional resources for further learning and encourage ongoing practice.	Books, online courses, webinars	-	10 weeks

CHAPTER 7

Creating Positive Change with a Growth Mindset

"Never doubt that a small group of thoughtful, committed citizens can change the world; indeed, it's the only thing that ever has."

-Margaret Mead

D O YOU REALIZE that adopting a growth mindset can influence many things? In this chapter, I will discuss how you can develop a growth mindset.

Becoming a Change Agent

Believe You Can Make an Impact through Purposeful Effort:

Believing you can make a difference by working hard can transform how you handle life's obstacles and opportunities. You must believe in your abilities and realize that every action may make a difference, no matter how tiny.

This concept holds that everything we do affects the world, even if we are unaware. Kindness, compassion, and dedication may help individuals in need, speak out for issues you believe in, or be there for someone struggling. Simply witnessing change is not enough to assume you can make a difference. To make a difference, it is necessary to act in difficult or ambiguous situations. This means using mistakes as opportunities to learn and failures as stepping stones to success.

Believing you can make a difference by focused effort affects others and yourself. Personal growth and discovery are possible when you live with conviction and purpose; being open to learning and personal growth opportunities strengthens you when things go wrong, helps you handle change, and enables you to overcome problems.

The belief that hard work can make a difference is a way of life; every day should be met with purpose since you know your actions can make a big impact. It means courageously taking risks and addressing obstacles, knowing you can change your life and others. The most important thing is to remember how powerful self-trust can be in making a lasting effect.

Educate Peers on Growth Principles:

Sharing your knowledge about growth principles with your peers can help you expand your reach and create positive change within your community. Recognizing the significance of spreading your development mindset knowledge is essential so that others can embrace personal growth and take meaningful steps toward achieving their goals. This remark emphasizes the importance of understanding growth mentality, the growth mindset popularized by psychologist Carol Dweck, who holds that hard work and dedication can improve intelligence. Teaching your peers about this principle gives them a robust framework for facing life's problems and opportunities with courage, passion, and a desire to learn and improve.

> *"The most important thing is to try and inspire people*
> *so that they can be great in whatever they want to do".*
> **-Kobe Bryant**

Informal discussions are a great approach to teaching peers about progress. Talking about your personal experiences helps explain a growth mindset. Sharing personal growth stories or discussing relevant research and literature in these casual conversations is the best way to learn and grow.

Classes and workshops offer structured opportunities to discuss growth principles. Talks and activities regarding the growth mindset in courses and shows can help students grasp how it pertains to their academic and personal lives. Formal learning events help schools foster a culture of learning and growth while teaching people. Leading by example is another effective technique for teaching growth ideas and fostering personal progress. You embody the growth mindset because you strive to improve yourself. Your actions, like going to school, developing new talents, or taking on new tasks, inspire others. Encouraging others to learn and collaborate can also help your community develop. Growth mindset lectures, seminars, and group projects allow people to learn from one another, share experiences, and grow together. These projects help people grasp growth concepts, build community, and empower everyone.

Set an Example of Lifelong Learning:

Leading by example and learning to help others shows your commitment to your improvement. It is about recognizing life's constant learning and progress as significant and sharing that journey to inspire others to grow and find their pathways. This point emphasizes the importance of lifelong learning and improvement. A degree is not enough; you need a curious, adaptable, and open-minded mentality. Learning new things throughout your life can improve your life and foster growth and creativity in your community and beyond.

Personal growth and development projects are great for teaching others lifelong learning. Attending school, taking classes, or participating in a professional development program sends a strong message to others. Aspiring others to prioritize their progress displays your dedication to self-improvement.

Continuous learning can significantly contribute to your personal and professional success. When you learn new things and improve your existing skills, you position yourself as a leader and innovator who can bring positive change to your community and society. By demonstrating your commitment to learning and personal growth, you can inspire and motivate others to strive for excellence in their own lives and careers. Being open to new ideas and perspectives is another critical component of learning. Understanding various cultures, ideas, and ways of thinking helps you understand the world and develop empathy. Being open to different ideas and perspectives improves your life and fosters a culture of acceptance and respect that values difference and lifelong learning to grow yourself collectively.

Inspiring Others Through Example

Leading by example is a solid technique for changing things since you may profoundly influence others' beliefs. By showing empathy, vulnerability, growth-focused leadership, and self-compassion, you can inspire and empower people beyond your circle.

Model Resilience and Self-Improvement in the Face of Setbacks:

Being positive and determined while mindful of how hard things are helps you recover from losses. We must accept that mistakes are inevitable and how we handle them affects our long-term growth. Showing perseverance shows others that issues are opportunities to grow personally and professionally.

Having a growth mentality implies seeing mistakes as learning opportunities rather than failures. Instead of dwelling on what went wrong, you focus on what you can learn and how to improve and become more resilient.

When you have this mindset, you inspire others to take failures as opportunities to improve. Your ability to recover from a loss shows how resilience and self-improvement may impact your life. Your strength inspires others to believe they can overcome any challenge.

Demonstrate Empathy, Vulnerability, and Growth Focused Leadership:

Vulnerability, empathy, and growth-focused leadership create a space where people feel supported, respected, and equipped to achieve. Creating a trusted, honest, and transparent culture inspires peers to collaborate, innovate, and grow.

Apply Principles with Compassion, including Self-Compassion:

Self-compassion is crucial to creating an accepting and caring environment. Respecting yourself means accepting your imperfections with compassion. This self-compassion creates strength, self-acceptance, and good mental health, which leads to personal progress and happiness. By practicing self-compassion, you can set an example for others to follow and learn the importance of treating oneself with kindness and understanding. When you are honest about your concerns and treat yourself with kindness and understanding, you create an environment where vulnerability is appreciated, mistakes are valuable learning opportunities, and self-care is vital to wellness.

Growth Mindset for Social Good

Many practical tools are available to help you employ a growth mindset, do nice things, and use these avenues to improve others' lives and the globe. Let's examine each option and how it might help you expand your abilities, resources, and drive.

Teaching Underprivileged Youth through Skills Workshops:

Through skills workshops, disadvantaged youngsters learn facts and get the courage to handle life's challenges and pursue their aspirations.

At these courses, you may transform lives by sharing your expertise, willingness to learn, and commitment to personal progress.

Skills workshops for teens and young adults are crucial to helping them believe in their abilities. These young individuals may come from places where they have little learning and growth opportunities. By offering skills classes, you empower them and teach them about themselves.

People who attend your classes can gain many essential skills for their personal and professional lives. You may help them improve their future by teaching them computer, coding, financial, or creative skills like art, music, or storytelling.

In addition to imparting technical skills, these classes help students grow personally and discover mentors. As a workshop leader, you can inspire and advise attendees to attain their goals. Sharing your opinions and lifelong experiences may help them know how to achieve their goals, even when facing formidable obstacles.

Teaching Underprivileged Youth through Skills Workshops

- Start with basic skills workshops in art, music, or coding to engage the youth.
- Provide a supportive and encouraging environment where participants feel safe to explore and learn.
- Incorporate interactive activities and hands-on projects to make learning enjoyable and practical.
- Foster a sense of teamwork and collaboration among the participants to encourage peer learning and support.
- Offer mentorship opportunities where skilled individuals can guide and inspire the youth to pursue their interests and goals.

Organizing skills classes for underprivileged teens helps them feel a connection to the community. These programs bring together teens and young adults from diverse backgrounds to learn, work, and collaborate. You assist people in gaining lifelong social and emotional skills by creating a welcoming, supportive, and opinion-valued environment.

Fundraising for Non-profits:

Fundraising for NGOs that aid poor areas is a powerful approach to promoting social good and positive change. By doing this, you can change the lives of people who struggle with education, employment, and personal growth.

Utilizing your networks to raise money is crucial. Because of your extensive connections, you can rally support for significant social issues and draw notice to them. Reaching out to friends, family, coworkers, and others helps boost fundraising.

Another way to raise money is by hosting events. A charity gala, fundraising show, or neighborhood bake sale allows NGOs to interact with contributors, share their vision, and generate funds. Planning, acquiring sponsors, and recruiting volunteers may create memorable events that raise money and support.

Mentorship Programs for Individual Potential:

- Pair mentees with mentors with relevant expertise and similar interests or career paths.
- Provide structured guidance and support to help mentees set and achieve realistic goals.
- Encourage regular communication and feedback sessions between mentors and mentees to facilitate growth and development.workplace failures.

Group fundraising is about increasing awareness and advocating for issues, not money. To boost your fundraising, bring attention to key social issues and advocate for fairness and inclusion policies and programs. In the long term, this will aid underprivileged groups.

Mentorship Programs for Individual Potential

Mentorship programs are a rewarding opportunity to help others improve personally and professionally. As a guide, you help your mentees solve problems, gain skills, and achieve their goals. Give your students guidance, support, and encouragement to transform their lives. They will have the tools to reach their potential and improve the world.

Mentoring is a great way to help others. This goes beyond advice to offer emotional support. A trusted confidant and a listening ear allow mentees to openly discuss anxieties, thoughts and objectives. Your empathy, support, and encouragement help mentees grow self-confidence and resilience. Sharing your opinions and experiences is essential. By sharing your struggles, accomplishments, and failures, you can help your mentees find their own path. Ideas and tips from your experience can help them see things differently and build the skills and mentality needed to solve problems and achieve their goals.

Grassroots Growth Campaigns

Here are some great ideas for starting a grassroots growth movement in your community to promote a growth mentality. These projects arm people of all ages with the skills and mindset to flourish individually and collectively. You can lead your community with these activism ideas:

Growth Mindset Workshops at Community Centers:

Organizing growth mindset classes at local community centers helps people and the community grow. These programs teach people of all ages how a growth mindset may alter their lives and help them overcome difficulties and confidently pursue their goals. Let us build on this idea to create meaningful growth mindset classes:

First, classes should be entertaining, interactive, and open to all ages and backgrounds. Activities, conversations, and tasks may suit varied learning styles and preferences, ensuring everyone can fully participate in and benefit from the workshop. Various ways exist to engage people and question their learning and growth beliefs. Group discussions, role-playing, hands-on activities, and reflective journals are examples.

Workshops should emphasize resilience, drive, and self-improvement. Stressing these notions empowers people to overcome obstacles and self-doubt and feel empowered and capable. Interactive presentations and real-life examples can demonstrate how people with a growth mindset solve difficulties. People like these are positive, tenacious, and prepared to learn from their mistakes.

Petitions for Growth Mindset Training:

Start petitions for growth mindset training in schools, companies, and communities to influence structural change. Get people to support resilience and adaptability and spread the word about growth mindset education.

First, explain the petition's goals and why growth mindset training is necessary. Drawing attention to research and proof that teaching a growth mindset can help students succeed in school, improve as individuals, and achieve good results in various situations helps strengthen the petition. Finding target groups and stakeholders who can implement growth mindset training courses is also crucial to the petition's success. Talking to decision-makers, including school officials, policymakers, human resources professionals, and community leaders, about the petition increases its chances of success and growth mindset programming. To maximize its influence, the petition should be promoted on multiple channels and signed by many people. Social media, petition sites, community forums, and traditional media can spread the cause and reach many people. You may convince others to sign and support the petition by carefully sharing facts, telling success stories, and encouraging community involvement. Supporting organizations, community partners, and like-minded organizations can help the petition reach more people and have a more significant impact. Unions and partnerships with like-minded groups help everyone work together and raise awareness of the petition. Sharing resources, expertise, and networks boosts advocacy and change.

Follow up on the petition by talking to lawmakers, decision-makers, and critical people to demand action and policy changes. This may involve meetings, letters, and lobbying efforts to ensure petition supporters' voices are heard in decision-making.

Key Takeaways

- Mindsets shape behaviors and norms
- Progress takes place through daily actions
- Lead through vulnerability and service
- Lift others up to realize their potential

Summary Action Plan:

Location	Issue to Address	Proposed Initiatives
School Library	Low engagement in learning	Book Club Initiatives: Start a book club that focuses on stories of personal development and overcoming challenges, encouraging discussions on growth and perseverance.
	Low engagement in learning	Growth Mindset Workshops: Organize workshops led by teachers or guest speakers to teach students about the growth mindset, including activities that reflect on failures as opportunities for growth.
		Interactive Learning Displays: Create displays around the library that showcase famous failures and successes in various fields (science, arts, sports, etc.), highlighting the importance of persistence and continuous learning.

CHAPTER 8

Sustaining a Growth Mindset

"We continue to grow as long as we are committed to it."
                                                    -Arturo Toscanini

A GROWTH MINDSET IS a way of thinking achieved over time by the need for commitment and community. In this chapter, you will get tips to keep your growth attitude throughout for long-term success.

Prioritizing Self-Care

Spending money on your health and happiness is important, but spending on your well-being also sets you up for long-term success; each part of self-care is essential for these reasons:

Sufficient Sleep Fuels Mind/Body Growth Capacity

Sleep is essential for your health, especially in today's fast-paced world; people prioritize work, fun, and socialization by mingling with others in place of taking rest and oversleeping. Sleep deprivation has a profound impact on the mind and body, which can be seen both in the long term and short term in the human body. Why is sleep important, and how does it grow your body and mind? Consider sleep your body's "reset button." It fixes, renews, and restores for the day.

During sleep, brains process information, build memories, and eliminate daytime toxins. Does a whole night's sleep improve your thinking? Yes, sleep is essential for the brain's overall health. Your brain operates less efficiently without proper sleep, making it harder to focus, learn, and remember. Sleep boosts memory, attentiveness, and problem-solving. Without sufficient sleep, education and work performance may suffer significantly.

More than your intellect, sleep improves your body, depicting the importance of sleep in your life. When you sleep, your body manufactures proteins, heals tissues, and releases growth hormones, muscle repair, immunity, and health, depending on this process. Lack of sleep lowers immunity, making you worse. Avoid sleep deprivation at all costs to avoid obesity, diabetes, heart disease, and other health issues.

Most sleep specialists recommend 7–9 hours of restful sleep every night, dimming the lights, deep breathing, meditation, or a warm bath, which can help you relax before bed.

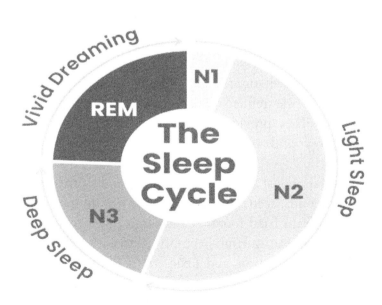

Good Nutrition Provides Building Blocks for Development

Food significantly impacts our health, growth, and development, which is reflected in the saying, "You are what you eat." Just as cars require fuel, our bodies need a balanced diet of nutrients to function and thrive. Considering our body as a complex mechanism that requires constant maintenance, we must ensure we consume a nutritious, nutrient-dense diet to support our needs. Getting enough lean protein helps muscles grow and recover. Amino acids from chicken, fish, tofu, and legumes build potent muscles. Protein fills you up, preventing overeating. Complex carbs in whole grains provide all-day energy, and fully processed grains contain fiber, vitamins, and minerals, while refined grains do not. They provide daylong energy and blood sugar control.

Nutrition Tips:

- Emphasize a balanced diet rich in fruits, vegetables, whole grains, lean proteins, and healthy fats to provide essential nutrients for growth and development.
- Educate people on the importance of hydration and encourage them to consume water throughout the day.
- Promote mindful eating habits, such as listening to hunger cues and avoiding excessive intake of processed foods high in sugars, salt, and unhealthy fats.

Healthy fats boost energy, cell growth, and nutrition absorption. Avocados, almonds, seeds, and olive oil are healthy fats; cut saturated and trans fats from fried foods. A diet high in processed foods, sugar, and bad fats is unhealthy. High in empty calories, these meals can trigger weight gain, inflammation, and toxic stress. Remember, obesity, heart disease, diabetes, and cancer can result from poor diets.

Watch your diet for nutrition. Five colorful fruit and vegetable servings daily are recommended. Eat lean proteins, whole grains, and healthy fats instead of processed and sugary foods. Menu planning and cooking beforehand help you stick to your diet for longer, and cooking at home gives you greater control and healthier eating.

Mental Health Supports Help Sustain Motivation

Your mental health affects your overall health and quality of life. It underpins your mental health, emotional strength, and relationships. Even while mental health is crucial, society ignores or shames it, making many people forget their emotional requirements. Taking care of your mental health goes beyond handling immediate issues; building mental toughness, self-awareness, and a good attitude gives you the strength to endure life's ups and downs gracefully.

Seeking Out Mentors and Allies

Here is why it is good to build ties with role models who are focused on growth:

Achievers Who Offer Wisdom and Accountability

Mentors can guide your career and personal growth. Successful people who have reached industry milestones are willing to share their expertise and experiences; they can help you organize your journey by sharing their experiences. Listening to their stories and soaking in what they say can teach you things that would take years to figure out.

Mentors also have a unique duty that can help you succeed. Knowing someone supports and believes in you might motivate you to accomplish your best. Mentors can give you mild pushes or timely notes to stay focused and on track. Their counsel can help you set achievable objectives, plan to achieve them, and keep your commitments.

Peers Mutually Committed to Improvement

People committed to personal and professional improvement might be like rocks in the ever-changing sea of life. While teachers can offer valuable perspectives, peers going through similar experiences can provide a unique support system that is both energizing and inspiring. Surrounding yourself with individuals dedicated to growth creates a supportive environment where you

Five Facts About Making a Commitment:

1. Every commitment is a choice.
2. Every commitment requires personal responsibility.
3. Every commitment requires honesty and integrity.
4. Every commitment is a promise.
5. Every commitment requires a choice. high in sugars, salt, and unhealthy fats.

can thrive. These peers share similar problems and accomplishments, fostering a strong sense of camaraderie and understanding. Peer relationships offer a distinct sense of belonging and understanding.

Your peers can support and aid you, having likely faced similar challenges themselves. They celebrate your successes and encourage you through your journey. However, peer interactions go beyond mere mental support and provide valuable learning and growth opportunities. Peers with diverse experiences and perspectives can offer new information and ideas, broadening your worldview and challenging your beliefs.

Coaches Who Encourage Measurable Progress

Coaches guide you personally and professionally, helping you navigate unfamiliar areas and stay on course. While mentors and peers are beneficial and enjoyable, coaches can provide targeted, results-oriented guidance based on your goals. Professional coaches specialize in assisting people to improve in specific areas or talents, unlike mentors who offer general guidance based on their own experiences. A coach can help you reach your potential with tailored feedback, techniques, and accountability, whether you aspire to lead, speak, or change jobs. Feedback and an outside perspective can pull you out of your comfort zone and help you overcome limiting assumptions. Find a teacher who is an expert in the subject you wish to improve and has helped others succeed. Look for coaches with certified coaching experience, client referrals, and positive reviews.

Building a Culture of Growth

It is not enough for individuals to create an atmosphere of growth; it is also essential to ensure everyone has the chance to learn, grow, and do well. Making growth-focused places together takes work and teamwork, whether at school, a club, or a community center. Here are some things you can do to help create these kinds of places:

Physical Spaces Designed for Collaboration

The physical environment affects how individuals act and interact. When designing areas for growth, it is important to prioritize items that facilitate collaboration, creativity, and communication. Examples include open floor plans, movable seating, brainstorming, and group workspaces. Tech and multimedia tools may make learning more enjoyable and help people share their knowledge. Interactive whiteboards, multimedia displays, and collaborative software can let diverse people collaborate.

Team Norms Valuing Trust, Vulnerability, and Effort

Team norms must prioritize trust, vulnerability, and effort to support progress. Successful teams and communities depend on trust, which allows people to work, communicate, and take risks without fear of repercussions. Encourage vulnerability by providing a friendly setting for sharing thoughts, feelings, and experiences. Create a culture of empathy, active listening, and constructive feedback that values everyone's voice.

Policies Enabling Continuous Education/Upskilling

Community and organizational rules and habits profoundly impact the workplace culture. Policies emphasizing continuing learning, skill-building, and professional development help people and the company or community succeed.

Creating policies that foster learning and skill-building delivers the message that everyone in the community or organization is respected and encouraged to learn. Businesses may help people succeed in today's fast-changing world by offering courses, training, and mentorship. Investing in educational programs that encourage learning benefits everyone, including the group or community; learning new things helps people remain ahead, adapt, and compete. Encouraging employees to pursue their passions can also foster innovation and success.

Reward people who strive for growth and development to foster excellence and ongoing improvement. Setting performance criteria and awards that encourage learning and development goals motivates workers to engage in their personal progress and demonstrates the firm's commitment to their professional advancement.

A growth-oriented culture requires everyone in an organization or group to collaborate and contribute. Organizations may facilitate teamwork, promote trust, openness, and hard work, and allow employees to keep learning and growing. This allows everyone to learn, grow, and succeed. Remember that developing a culture of growth takes time, dedication, and a shared goal of success for everyone.

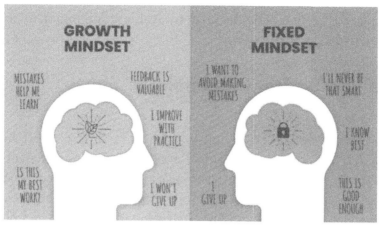

Daily Meditation or Journaling

For centuries, mindfulness meditation has helped people be more present and aware. Present-mindedness is key. Visualization of body scans and focused breathing can help. Attention to the present can help you relax, reduce stress, and find peace.

Meditation for even a short time daily can improve mental and emotional health. Morning meditation can set a positive tone for the day; afternoon meditation can center your mind and relax your body. Either way, meditation will help you recharge and refocus amid daily stress.

Meditation Tips:

- Set aside a specific time for meditation or journaling each day to establish a consistent practice.
- Create a comfortable, quiet space free from distractions to enhance focus and relaxation during meditation or journaling sessions.
- Experiment with different meditation techniques or journaling prompts to find what resonates best with you and supports your mental well-being

Try different meditation techniques and write activities in your diary to determine what works best for you. Some people like organized or guided meditation, while others like more free-form or creative methods.

It is essential to find activities that are real and important to you and promise to do them every day.

Unplugging from Technology

In today's fast-paced digital environment, it is easy to become addicted to devices. We constantly receive notifications, emails, and social media updates on our phones, laptops, tablets, and wearables. Technology has transformed our lives, employment, and relationships, but too much time online can harm our mental, emotional, and physical health. Setting aside "screen-free" times or zones in our homes helps us unplug from technology. Making the bedroom and dining room tech-free could entail banning technology. Screen-free periods like meals and bedtime might help us disconnect from our devices and be more present.

Disconnecting from technology goes beyond turning off devices. It also involves doing things that make us feel mentally well. Instead of browsing social media or binge-watching Netflix, spend time outdoors with loved ones or doing activities that make you happy. Spending time with loved ones can also help alleviate the loneliness and detachment caused by too much computer usage. Dining with family, having coffee with friends, or having a family game night can enhance our ties and connect us.

Self-Compassion Exercises

Meditation involves repeating kind words to oneself and others, promoting self-compassion and empathy. Self-compassion can be developed by confronting negative self-talk, recognizing mistakes as learning opportunities, and forgiving and accepting yourself.

Key Takeaways

- Self-care prevents burnout and renews motivation
- Mentors provide wisdom, accountability, and encouragement
- Surround yourself with others committed to growth
- Uphold growth mindset values despite difficulties

Summary Action Plan:

Action Item	Details	Timeline
Arrange periodic meetings with a mentor	Schedule regular meetings with a mentor who embodies a growth mindset to receive guidance and accountability.	Every 90 days
Establish 90-day growth goals	Set specific, measurable, and realistic growth goals to discuss and review with your mentor.	Every 90 days
Check progress and realign goals	Review the progress toward the set goals with your mentor and make adjustments as necessary.	Every 90 days
Prioritize self-care	Regularly engage in activities that promote mental, physical, and emotional health.	Daily
Foster a supportive environment	Surround yourself with peers and mentors committed to growth, creating a mutual support and learning culture.	Ongoing
Invest in continuous learning	Participate in educational programs and upskilling opportunities to stay competitive and innovative.	Ongoing
Practice mindfulness and meditation	Incorporate daily practices of meditation or journaling to enhance focus and mental clarity.	Daily
Unplug from technology	Designate screen-free times and zones in your life to reduce digital distractions and improve presence.	Daily
Engage in self-compassion exercises	Regularly perform exercises that foster self-compassion to nurture a positive self-image and resilience.	Daily
Build and adhere to a nutritious diet	Plan and consume a balanced diet rich in proteins, whole grains, and healthy fats.	Daily
Maintain a regular sleep schedule	Ensure 7–9 hours of quality sleep each night to support overall health and cognitive function.	Daily

CHAPTER 9

Envisioning Your Growth Mindset Future

"The future belongs to those who believe in the beauty of their dreams."

-Eleanor Roosevelt

WHEN YOU COMMIT to lifelong growth and learning, you open yourself up to incredible possibilities! This chapter will help you envision the incredible future within your reach by envisioning your growth mindset.

Reflecting on Growth Thus Far

Reflect on your growth which has happened so far and see how you can further improve it by reading the steps given below:

1. Review Journals Detailing Key Lessons and Insights

Looking through your journals is like touring your head; it will expose rich emotions and thoughts. Each page depicts a growth period and offers helpful information and lessons. These words, written in a notebook or a digital journal, hold your life experiences and document your path.

When reading your journals, remember recurring themes and significant events that defined your trip; these insights will reveal your strengths, limitations, and growth areas. When things are unknown, you may have more self-doubt and uncertainty or be lured to challenging undertakings. These observations reveal how your mind operates, telling us the thoughts and ideas that influence your actions and choices. Your notebook is a chance to express thanks for the small victories and joyous moments that give your life value. Please consider the warmth of a loved one's embrace or the beauty of a pink and gold sunset. When life gets tough, gratitude may remind you of daily beauty and plenty around you.

Write more in your book and cherish the ideas and lessons you have learned. Enjoy changing and growing and use challenges to discover more about yourself.

2. Assessment Tests: Tracking Competency Progress

Assessment tests are more than merely stopovers; they effectively benchmark your growth. Academic, work, and skill assessments are essential milestones that reflect your growth as you approach assessment tests with an open mind. See them as opportunities to reflect on your development rather than challenges. Review these tests and note what you did well and what you could improve.

Self-Reflection:

- Allocate dedicated time for self-reflection, preferably at the end of each day or week, to review your experiences, emotions, and actions.
- Ask yourself open-ended questions during self-reflection sessions to delve deeper into your thoughts and behaviors, facilitating personal growth and self-awareness.

Assessment tests are not just about revealing your strengths; they also provide valuable feedback that can guide your future growth. When you receive positive feedback, be proud of your accomplishments and grateful for your perseverance.

Celebrate your progress and achievements, whether passing an exam, receiving favorable performance evaluation comments, or proving your worth.

Remember, evaluation tests can also highlight areas for improvement. However, instead of seeing this as a sign of failure, view feedback as a valuable resource.

It is a stepping stone for growth, a tool that can help you improve in the future. Ask yourself: What can I learn from this? How can I use this feedback to become even better?

Every test is a chance for you to learn and grow. Reflect on your performance, identify areas for improvement, and take proactive steps to address them. This could mean seeking more training or tools, exploring new talents, or reaching out for support from mentors or peers. By embracing each test as a learning opportunity, you set yourself up for continuous growth and development.

3. Gratitude Mindfulness for Abilities Cultivated

The power of mindfulness may improve your life. It might uplift your spirit and satisfy you; it involves reflecting on and being thankful for all the positive things in your life, especially your abilities, knowledge, and personal growth.

The world moves swiftly and disorderly; we can get caught up in regular life and overlook the countless gifts and opportunities around us. Practicing gratitude mindfulness daily will help you appreciate what you have accomplished more. First, reflect on your daily skill gains and celebrate your development and improvement, whether it is a skill you have practiced for years, a talent you have worked hard at, or a quality you have cultivated through self-reflection and analysis. Feel happy and prosperous for your accomplishments.

4. Setting New Horizons:

Your next journey begins on the verge of new challenges. Now is the moment to imagine the future. To achieve your goals successfully, embrace your sense of purpose from your growth path and set new limitations. Create a broader vision for yourself, see your ideal self in five years, and develop goals that match your hobbies and purpose to expand your ambitions.

1. Destination Vision Boards:

Destination vision boards are effective in turning fantasies into goals. Think of each item on your vision board as a colorful patchwork of your ideal existence. Gather photos, phrases, and other items that reflect your dreams. These might be photographs of places you want to visit, words that make you happy, or symbols of your beliefs. Let your imagination run wild, and let your instincts tell you which sections call to you. You can travel and explore different cultures and activities; your vision board may include photographs of distant places, stunning countryside, and active cities. Each photo reminds you of the excitement waiting for you and the awe and wonder of new things.

Destination vision boards go beyond work goals and include personal growth and happiness goals. Whether you are developing meaningful relationships, expressing your creativity, or prioritizing your health, your vision board represents your ideal existence. Adding photos and symbols of your aspirations to your vision board will help you grow and change. After gathering your pictures and signs, create your vision board. Use your imagination to move and modify pieces to create a composition that speaks to you. Making a vision board has no rules. Follow your instincts and let your creativity create a meaningful design. Keep your vision board visible so you can view it daily.

2. Imagining Your Best Self in 5 Years:

Imagine your finest self-standing, tall, confident, radiating purpose, grinning warmly. How do they walk? Do you move gracefully, exuding quiet confidence that reflects inner strength and resilience? Consider what your best self has accomplished in the past five years. They may have advanced in their jobs and are eager to take on more tasks. They may have studied or trained more to pursue their ambitions, supported by friends and family who celebrate their success and help them when needed.

What makes up your best self goes beyond your accomplishments and encompasses your entire being. Consider how your abilities, values, and hobbies have shaped your five-year journey. Your empathy and compassion may have improved, making it easier to connect with others. You may have discovered new hobbies and interests that give you daily purpose and motivation.

Imagine having a meaningful life and improving the world at your best. Watch them enjoy themselves by volunteering, creating, or spending time with loved ones. Imagine them addressing problems with courage and confidence, knowing every struggle is an opportunity to grow.

3. Exploring Goals Aligned with Core Interests/Purpose:

Your hobbies, passions, and ideas define you and guide your life. These core activities and purposes are the guiding stars for life's direction and meaning. As you face life's obstacles, developing goals that reflect your interests and values is crucial. Self-awareness and contemplation are the first stages in choosing goals that match your passions. Think about what makes you happy and fulfilled, then include these things in your plans and goals. Be guided by your purpose; it might be a career you love, a cause you care about, or soulful relationships.

Setting goals that align with your values requires careful consideration and focus on goals that reflect who you are and what you stand for rather than what others think or what society says is right. Consider how your goals will affect your satisfaction and sense of success and prioritize those that align with your values and aspirations.

If environmental protection is essential to you, you may make goals about sustainability and eco-friendliness. This could involve promising to reduce your carbon footprint, supporting environmental groups, or advocating for conservation laws. Matching your objectives with your ecological concerns helps a cause you care about and makes you feel fulfilled and purposeful. Suppose you are passionate about art and self-expression. Set goals for creative undertakings. This could entail taking art classes, blogging, YouTube streaming, or entering local art shows. You can improve your work and inspire others by seizing opportunities to express yourself.

Fulfilling Your Potential:

Realizing your full potential is not a goal but a journey that never ends, an adventure that starts with constant learning and growth. As you begin this journey, remember that growth does not stop at a certain point in time. It is an ongoing process that changes over time based on your interest, drive, and sense of purpose. Let us talk about how learning new things throughout your life, the fact that this adventure never ends, and the fact that your purpose changes over time affect your quest to reach your full potential.

Growth Through Lifelong Learning:

Learning new things and widening one's worldview drive human growth, as lifelong learning displays curiosity and a desire to progress. It transcends formal schooling, classrooms, and texts; it involves discovery and investigation. A commitment to personal and intellectual growth is excellent for the mind and heart.

Take A Coffee Break!
You must be tired of reading this book and starting to feel sleepy. Take a sip of coffee, take a little break, and come back again to get more valuable insights into your interests and career options in the next sections of the book.

Continuous learning helps people adapt to change, which is great. Because the world is continually changing, learning and growing enables you to navigate modern life.

Learning throughout life helps people accept change and see it as an opportunity to improve. Exploring and knowing about new things helps lifelong learners handle new situations, solve difficulties, and seize opportunities to improve personally and professionally.

Learning new things throughout your life can help you grow and discover yourself, as new ideas, perspectives, and ways of thinking will constantly challenge your beliefs as you grow.

As you mature mentally and emotionally, you become more self-aware and understand the world.

It challenges your beliefs and attitudes, and you embrace human complexity with humility.

This activity can improve your life significantly, like learning a language or instrument, or the beauty of nature makes you joyful, gives you purpose, and makes you feel like you are making a difference. Learners who love their hobbies and interests find motivation and value in learning.

This Is a Perpetual Adventure, not a Final Destination:

Your journey to discover your potential transcends time and space, and this path of self-discovery and growth is never-ending and is distinguished by change and growth.

Remember that the secret to unlocking your potential is not reaching a certain point but welcoming the process with open arms and a continuing sense of wonder and excitement. To unlock your potential, you must accept that success is only judged by external accomplishments or milestones.

Instead, it is about finding enjoyment and satisfaction in learning and growing as a person and seeing every moment as an opportunity to learn and explore. This adventure will include challenges and times when you question your course. These challenges may appear daunting, yet they build your strength and resilience. Accept them as necessary milestones to realize your best potential, recognizing that difficulty is when you grow most.

Maintain your guts and drive when things get tough; remember that failures are diversions that might lead to discoveries and insights, so be resilient, confident in your capacity to overcome obstacles, and persevere.

Above all, remember that the vacation is fantastic; the goal is to fully and actively appreciate the process of growth and self-discovery. Enjoy the small victories and milestones. Each step advances your potential toward your journey, and unlocking your potential requires courage, perseverance, and curiosity. Be open to opportunities and believe in the ability of growth and self-discovery to change your life, as unlimited opportunities exist.

Your Purpose Will Evolve as Your Interests Expand

The force of having goals that are interlinked with your interests is like a bright light that guides you and gives your life significance despite shifting circumstances. Your purpose evolves as you attain your potential and discover your passions. It is natural and lovely, showing how your most significant goals and dreams have developed like a seedling becoming an oak tree.

Your mission blossoms unexpectedly.

It would help if you were curious, open to new ideas, and willing to learn to accept change. Rather than being tied to a purpose, let your passions guide you. Always follow your emotions and trust your intuition to find new opportunities and methods. Maintaining your ideals and ambitions is crucial. These stabilize you while things shift. These ideas guide you and explain life's complexities. As your purpose changes, let your values guide you and keep you accurate to yourself. Learning to shift and adapt is crucial when you realize that your meaning is changing. You should be ready to modify your course like a sailor changing sails to catch the wind. Remember that the road to self-discovery is winding and full of bends. Every detour and turnoff contributes to your life's colorful journey, so use them to learn and grow.

Paying it Forward:

You can pay it forward by teaching others about the power of a growth mindset as you continue to learn more about yourself and grow. Sharing your knowledge and experiences can start a suitable chain reaction that encourages people of all ages to take on tasks, keep going even when things go wrong, and reach their full potential. Let us talk about specific ways you can share the ideas of a growth mindset and encourage others to start their paths of change.

1. Giving Presentations to Younger Kids:

When standing in front of a classroom full of curious, interested students and younger kids, talks are a chance to teach them and create seeds of courage and resolve that will bloom as they age.

Make your lectures engaging and hands-on to engage these young brains and spark their imaginations. Use concrete examples and hands-on activities to explain the development mindset, and use chores, games, and role-playing to make learning fun and memorable. Tell stories demonstrating the importance of hard effort, perseverance, and strength to succeed. Kids should learn that mistakes are regular and valuable and show them that making errors is a sign of trying new things and aiming to be the best. Encourage kids to believe they can control their lives and achieve anything with hard effort and perseverance.

Talking to younger kids helps them develop lifelong attributes like strength and persistence. You educate kids about the growth mindset and equip them to become firm, confident people who do not fear trying new things and passionately pursuing their dreams.

2. Starting Growth Mindset Clubs:

Imagine entering a room full of eager faces with a strong sense of purpose and drive. Growth mindset clubs are a unique way to unite people who want to create a culture of growth and strength; friendships can grow beyond boundaries when members support, encourage, and advise each other in open and honest conversations.

Starting growth mindset clubs requires planning workshops, discussions, and events. Consider holding workshops on growth mindset topics like goal setting, resilience, and self-talk, giving members tools and tips to develop a growth mindset and solve problems.

Lead conversations where people can express their thoughts, feelings, and ideas about matters that affect personal growth and development. As members put the concepts they have learned into practice in their own lives, they become growth mindset advocates who spread inspiration and happiness to those around them. By starting growth mindset clubs, you may build a beneficial group where individuals can get together to learn, progress, and support each other on their personal and professional development paths.

By encouraging a culture of growth and strength, you start a chain reaction that makes other people want to use the power of a growth mindset in their own lives; this makes the future better and stronger for everyone.

3. Creating Instructional Social Media Content:

Social networking is a tremendous connecting method in today's busy digital world. This virtual stage lets people exchange ideas, start movements, and change their lives. As the digital world evolves, educational videos on YouTube and Facebook can communicate growth mindset principles to a large, diverse audience across cultures and boundaries.

Instagram, YouTube, and TikTok offer unique opportunities to foster strength and motivation. Unlike any other, these platforms allow you to connect with individuals from diverse backgrounds and across the globe. Leveraging social media to share your message and initiate a global dialogue about the growth mindset can be life changing. Educational social media content is all about breaking down complex topics into bite-sized, memorable pieces such as short films, infographics, and blog posts that can quickly capture attention and invite active participation.

Imagine developing a short film about overcoming obstacles and persevering; animation, commentary, and visual storytelling may bring these ideas to life for your audience. Add questions that make you think and reflect to encourage individuals to consider how they handle challenges.

Infographics are another attractive method of displaying data; using images, charts, and text, you can create visuals demonstrating the benefits of a growth mindset and offer advice on resilience and determination. People can store, share, and refer to these photos to remember their lessons. Social media material may educate, inspire, and motivate, so share inspiring stories of hardworking people who overcame obstacles and achieved greatness. By showcasing real-life examples of growth mindset use, you demonstrate to your audience that they can overcome obstacles and achieve their goals. Thought-provoking questions, valuable recommendations, and motivational success stories can help your audience feel connected. Asking them about their difficulties and experiences will foster learning and growth in a safe environment.

Social media can help you convey that hard work and devotion can improve your talents. Instructional social media material can pique the audience's curiosity and inspire possibility, empowering them to reach their potential and begin their growth and self-discovery. As we conclude our exploration of the growth mindset, let's recap the core concepts and commit to applying these powerful principles in our daily lives.

Key Takeaways

- Reflect on progress made and lessons learned
- Allow your dreams to expand
- Set bold goals aligned with your purpose
- Your growth story is just beginning

Exercise:

Summary Action Plan

Write a letter to your future self-envisioning who you will become by embracing the growth mindset principles covered in this book

Your Letter

CHAPTER 10

Living the Growth Mindset

"Knowing is not enough; we must apply. Wishing is not enough; we must do."

-Johann Wolfgang von Goethe

WE'VE COVERED A lot of ground on the growth mindset journey! This final chapter will recap the key takeaways so you can start living these principles today, review the core concepts to find out what works best for you and act accordingly.

Core Concepts Review

Here, you will review some key concepts that will teach you some important life lessons that are going to be helpful in your personal and professional life:

Abilities are Flexible and Can Grow with Effort over Time

Call your skills a large garden full of potential waiting for your attentive care; you can develop your skills and talents like a good gardener nurtures their plants. Greatness grows from hard work, practice, and persistence.

Remembering that our abilities are naturally malleable is extremely important in a world with fixed skills. We can easily give up on the idea that we're born with a particular skill and can do nothing else, which is not valid, as you can develop every ability you have, whether it's an instrument, a sport, or your career. A growth mindset drives this change, as it's the concept that if you work hard and are willing to try new things, you can improve your skills. Reflect on your personal experience and your concerns and issues when starting something new. You may have felt unprepared, uncertain, or too busy to undertake the massive task, but you made progress with each try, failure, and modest step forward.

Growth is about slow, gradual change. Like a seedling growing through the ground to reach the sun, your skills can increase with the appropriate conditions. It involves accepting the process, relishing the small triumphs, and believing in your ability to adjust and adapt.

To progress, you must be involved and willing to leave your comfort zone, not merely optimistic. It implies tackling challenges head-on, even if the path is scary or uncertain, and actively seeking learning and growth opportunities, whether from formal education, a mentor, or many different settings.

Growth occurs in collaborative, supportive situations. Join others who want to grow and will help you become the greatest. Support each other and learn from others who have gone through the same.

You can accomplish anything in your talent garden. Patience, persistence, and self-confidence can help you reach new heights in your skills and capabilities. Maintain your yard, water it, and watch it blossom into a gorgeous success and happiness.

Learn from Setbacks through Adjustment and Perseverance

Failures, those unpleasant guests on the path to achievement, often appear unexpectedly. They can be missed opportunities, failed projects, or personal disappointments. How we handle challenges makes our routes unique, not the problems themselves; problems offer us a unique opportunity to learn, grow, and improve.

Consider a former failure that depressed you. It may have been a missed raise or a failed project. Maybe it was a personal loss, like an unexpected breakup or a dream that didn't come true. When disappointed, you may experience sadness, rage, or irritation. Failures are only stops on the path to success, so don't give up. Having a growth mindset helps overcome obstacles. We can use the loss to learn and grow instead of seeing it as a reflection of our badness. Ask, "What can I learn from this?" How can I improve from this loss? Thinking of loss as a step forward allows us to persevere when circumstances get tough.

Resilience and the ability to bounce back after a loss are not innate; these skills can be improved over time. You must improve and become more resilient after the storm. Resilience requires adapting to new situations, persevering, and finding meaning in our experiences.

Reflecting on your actions strengthens resilience. Examine your failures to learn what went wrong; you may have discovered a vulnerability or decided to adjust your habits. Thinking about our failures can help us evolve as humans. Being resilient requires hope and positivity, as well as thinking. Instead of dwelling on past mistakes, one must consider future possibilities. Make strategies and take action to achieve your goals. Have people who support you and help you succeed because support and encouragement from others strengthen you from the inside.

Progress Takes Patience and Self-Compassion

Waiting may seem like an unnecessary luxury in today's fast-paced world. Our society expects things to happen quickly and for our strenuous efforts to pay off, whereas real growth takes patience, tenacity, and self-compassion.

Being patient and understanding that change takes time are critical. For success, I suggest running, not sprinting. There will be times of excitement and fatigue, but persistent work gets you through, so always enjoy the journey and each step and trust the process.

Self-compassion and patience are essential for growth. The gentle voice reminds us to be nice to ourselves, especially in difficult times. Instead of being hard on yourself, be kind and compassionate like a close friend going through a trying moment. Remember that mistakes are part of being human. Don't blame yourself for falling or getting off track on your vacation. Instead, acknowledge your sadness, anger, strength, and growth. Mistakes teach us about ourselves and make us stronger and more resilient. Making progress is about the journey, with all its ups and downs; as you develop and change, you must trust that you can handle the challenges. When you're impatient or self-conscious, breathe deeply and keep calm. Recognize your development, even if you can't see it, and celebrate your minor victories and progress toward your goals.

Turning Insights into Action

After learning about growth and resilience, apply what you've learned; remember that even a little time spent following these guidelines daily might help you improve tremendously. Let's discuss how to shift your mindset, create new habits, and enjoy becoming more substantial and robust.

Implement Small Mindset Shifts Consistently

Daily changes in thinking can affect our lives, and small changes in how we think about and solve everyday situations can lead to substantial emotional growth. By making little changes, we can establish a growth attitude that helps us solve difficulties positively and resiliently.

You can modify your mindset by seeing obstacles as opportunities to progress and making challenges stepping stones to progress rather than obstacles. This mindset change helps us learn from failures and persevere when things get tough as we reach our most significant potential and can manage any obstacle when we feel our talents can be improved with hard work and determination.

> *"Every day brings new choices."*
>
> -Martha Beck

Constancy is critical when making tiny mental adjustments; you must make these modifications consistently until they become habits. This could involve drafting lists to recall ourselves, journaling about our experiences, or asking friends and family who value personal growth for aid. As we practice these positive thinking adjustments, we'll tackle challenges with more confidence and strength, increasing success and enjoyment in all aspects of our lives.

Build Habits Aligned with a Growth Mentality

Small changes in thinking can affect our lives, and these small changes in how we think about and solve everyday situations can lead to substantial emotional growth. By making little changes, we can establish a growth attitude that helps us solve difficulties positively and resiliently.

Accepting "yet" can also change your mind. Adding this tiny term to our vocabulary can transform our outlook on life. When goals seem impossible, saying, "I can't do this is easy." By adding "yet" at the end, we confess we have flaws but hope to improve. "I can't play the guitar" becomes "yet." This little addition gives us hope and energy by focusing on future successes rather than failures.

When making tiny mental adjustments, constancy is critical. You must consistently make these modifications until they become habits. This could involve drafting lists to recall ourselves, journaling about our experiences, or asking friends and family who value personal growth for aid. As we practice these positive thinking adjustments, we'll tackle challenges with more confidence and strength, increasing success and enjoyment in all aspects of our lives.

Celebrate Attempts and Wins, Focusing on Enjoyment

Honoring your successes and attempts helps you grow. Rewarding efforts and victories is crucial to feeling happy and driven, no matter how modest. By focusing on the process rather than the outcome, we can enjoy the journey and be proud of our tiny progress.

Imagine starting a career path; many challenges and setbacks await you. Instead of letting these issues depress you, admire your courage and determination to achieve your goals.

Celebrate your courage to leave your comfort zone and act no matter what, as failures are opportunities to learn and grow, which builds resilience and strength in times of adversity. Regardless of results, celebrating your attempts is a powerful approach to remind yourself of your commitment to growth. Each attempt demonstrates that you are willing to push yourself and understand that the journey may be unpredictable, so praise for your work enhances your confidence in your ability to solve difficulties and achieve goals no matter what.

When you reach a milestone or finish a task, celebrate your success because it demonstrates growth and progress; minor wins should be celebrated.

Give yourself a treat, tell your family about your success, or ponder about your hard work.

Including celebrations in your growth and resilience journey fosters gratitude and appreciation. It helps you enjoy the road and avoid focusing on the end objective. Accepting the good and bad of the journey enables you to discover your strengths and limitations, making you more robust and flexible when bad things happen.

Making Progress Daily

Maintaining personal progress and grit requires daily routines; by doing and thinking about your goals daily, you may establish a growth mindset and keep advancing toward them. Try daily writing, weekly competency assessments, and monthly self-care check-ins to grow and be kind to yourself.

Daily Journaling: Detailing Growth Efforts and Reflections

Write down your growth attempts and experiences in a notepad every morning and journal your successes and mistakes to learn about yourself and reflect. These tips in the box will help you write your book daily:

- Record your little steps to achieving your goals and celebrate your progress, whether learning a new skill, overcoming a fear, or leaving your comfort zone.
- Record any daily challenges, and consider how these issues taught you how to improve and become more resilient.
- Be kind and encouraging to yourself, and accept that failure is typical and part of learning.
- Daily journaling will help you understand your growth and become stronger over time.

Weekly Assessments of Competency Improvements

Track how your essential abilities have improved after each week to assess your growth. Choose goal-related topics to work on and utilize objective measurements or self-evaluations to track your progress.

1. Set clear, achievable weekly goals by dividing huge goals into smaller tasks and creating success criteria.
2. Assess your talents and abilities to achieve your goals. Performance metrics, peer or mentor input, and self-assessment tools can measure success.

3. This week, consider your accomplishments and areas for improvement. Be proud of your achievements and mindful of your weaknesses. Look at successful strategies and find methods to improve.

4. After considering them, change your weekly plans and methods and use your experiences and opinions to set new or improve previous goals.

You'll stay accountable to your goals and improve your methods by giving yourself weekly feedback.

Monthly Self-Care Check-Ins on Motivation/Burnout

As you concentrate on your profession and personal progress, prioritize your health to avoid burnout. Monthly self-checks can keep you motivated and assertive. By scheduling self-care check-ins, you'll build resilience and avoid burnout, helping you stay on your growth path.

- Assess Your Motivation: Consider your overall motivation and excitement about your goals. Consider your positive and negative emotions. Look for fatigue or burnout and act immediately.
- Recharge: Schedule monthly time for soul-nourishing activities. Relax and care for yourself by spending time in nature, practicing mindfulness, or creating.
- Seek assistance from friends, family, and teachers. Discuss your issues and triumphs and ask for help. Remember, you're not alone in life. Asking for aid shows strength.
- Alter Your Goals: Assess your duties and goals to see if you need to change to maintain balance. Be ready to say "no" to things or people who won't help you grow.

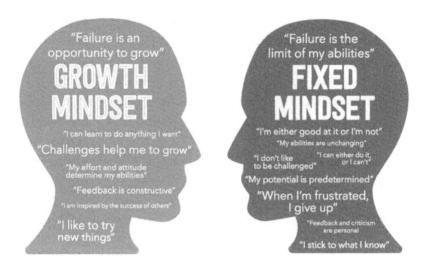

Lifelong Learning Journey

Consider the lives of people with growth mindsets who conquered problems by working hard as you start your lifelong learning journey. They include inventors, scientists, and ordinary people who achieved greatness, and their stories can inspire you to keep growing your growth attitude.

Famous Creators, Scientists, and Activists

History is replete with examples of people with a growth mentality who strive to learn more, innovate, and change the world. Famous artists, scientists, and activists have changed the globe. Their perseverance and commitment to greatness have inspired generations.

Famous personalities like Thomas Edison are associated with hard work and creative ideas.

Edison said, "I have not failed. I've just found 10,000 ways that won't work," which describes his unwavering belief in perseverance. Edison persevered to create the light bulb despite several setbacks. He tried different things and improved his ideas until he got it correctly. His tenacity and dedication led to one of the most revolutionary inventions, revolutionizing how we live, work, and interact. Marie Curie's tale shows how being curious, daring, and eager to learn can be powerful. Curie was a prominent scientist; her radioactive findings advanced modern physics and chemistry. Curie persevered despite discrimination as a woman scientist in a male-dominated field; her insatiable curiosity and commitment to improving scientific learning drove her. Her innovative research earned her two Nobel Prizes, making her a STEM role model for women.

Campaigner Malala Yousafzai shows how to be brave, strong, and always dedicated to justice. As a child, she risked her life to fight for girls' education in Pakistan, where extremist groups threatened her. Malala refused to be quiet despite the risk. She campaigned against injustice and inspired hope, strength, and resilience. Global recognition of her daring struggle earned her the Nobel Peace Prize. She represents courage and strength to millions.

Peers Who Overcame Obstacles Through Perseverant Effort

Famous people intrigue us, but stories about everyday stars among our peers do, too; these folks overcome significant obstacles to achieve their goals through tenacity and drive. Their stories may not be in history books, but their grit and dedication illustrate that greatness can be found in daily situations.

Single mother Sarah shows how crucial it is to stay going when things get tough; she raised her small children alone when her marriage dissolved unexpectedly. She risked attending college while working numerous jobs to improve her family's future. Sarah worked long hours, struggled with money, and tried to balance her obligations as a mother, student, and worker; there were days when she feared she might pass out from fatigue and doubted her ability to succeed.

Against all odds, Sarah's efforts paid off, and she graduated college with honors, demonstrating her hard work and dedication. She continued her journey. With her new qualifications, she got a promising career that fulfilled her family's needs and allowed her to grow. These anecdotes demonstrate that a growth mentality is for more than just the gifted. Hard work, determination, and a drive to learn and improve may create it in anyone. We should celebrate our peers' successes to honor the human spirit and learn from their deeds as we pursue our goals.

Avenues for Continued Learning

If you want to keep learning throughout your life, find ways to improve. Many resources and possibilities can aid your research and self-improvement. Consider these options:

1. Coursera, edX, and Udemy provide online courses and workshops on business, technology, art, and personal growth. Online learning makes gaining new skills or improving your understanding of a subject easy.

2. Learn and acquire ideas from books and podcasts. Read everything you like, from science fiction and biography to self-help and psychology. Join a book club or study group to discuss the book and learn new things.

3. Many organizations offer workshops and programs to help employees advance. Take advantage of these opportunities to learn, network, and keep current in your field.

4. Local adult education centers and community schools provide seminars and workshops on language learning, cuisine, gardening, and photography. These workshops offer a secure place to learn and meet like-minded people.

Find mentors and peers for guidance, support, and encouragement. Attend networking events, professional groups, and mentoring programs to expand your network and learn from others.

You know what to accomplish and have the means to succeed. We hope you enjoy lifelong learning and growth!

Key Takeaways

- Review growth mindset fundamentals
- Incremental progress compounds over time
- Apply principles consistently with self-compassion
- Live and lead with a growth mentality

Summary Action Plan:

30-Day Growth Mindset Progress Chart Example:

Day	Mantra Repeated (Yes/No)	Daily Reflections & Insights	Significant Progress
1	Yes	Felt more positive about challenges at work.	Noticed a shift in how I approach work tasks.
2	Yes	Reminded myself during a tough project.	Helped maintain focus and persistence.
3	Yes	Used it to motivate myself during a workout.	Workout felt easier with a positive mindset.
4			
5			
6			

CONCLUSION

IF YOU'RE TIRED of feeling stuck in your personal or professional life, this book will teach you how to adopt a growth mindset! With practical advice and inspiring ideals, you can transform yourself through hard work, persistence, and a strong belief in your ability to grow. As a special bonus, I want to thank you for reading this book to the end. To help you remember the most important points covered in this chapter, check out the key takeaways below. Happy reading!

Key Takeaways

1. You now know that abilities can be grown with hard work and determination. This book demonstrates that believing your skills may improve will help you tackle problems with hope and drive, whether your goals are school, sports, career, or personal. So, rather than being in a fixed mindset, try to improve yourself by having a growth mindset and knowing that nothing is innate. Instead, you can improve and build your muscle memory by consistently learning and practicing a new skill.

2. Challenges teach us that our problems are opportunities to learn and grow, not obstacles. Don't consider mistakes or difficulties failures. Consider them learning opportunities. Thinking this attitude can help you stay going and improve, helping you attain your goals.

3. Be patient and kind to yourself to progress: Setbacks are part of the journey, and personal improvement may take time. This book tells you to be friendly to yourself and compassionate when

things go wrong. Instead of giving up, use a short-term issue to learn something that will aid you.

4. Hang out with growth-minded folks. Your surroundings are crucial to a growth mindset. Spend time with growth-minded, encouraging people. They will motivate you, boost your confidence, and offer guidance. A support group will keep you accountable and inspired.

Embracing a Growth Mindset: An Inspirational Story

High school student Jake Thompson, who was 15 years old, struggled with studies and friends. He constantly compared himself to his peers, who performed well in school and extra-curriculars. He doubted himself and felt horrible. Jake was stressed because his parents had great expectations of him.

Jake's grades dropped significantly as his anxieties grew, and he stopped trying new things for fear of failure. This mentality caused him to withdraw from friends and feel lonely; he continued to criticize himself, making him feel worse, which was a clear sign of a negative mentality.

After he found a book about growth attitudes, his life changed. Hearing about others who overcame comparable issues shifted Jake's perspective. Problems didn't worry him anymore since he used them to learn and grow.

Jake found role models, such as his school teacher, Mr. Rodriguez, who believed in him. Inspired by this support, Jake adopted a growth mindset, which led him to study more effectively and work harder. As his grades improved, Jake felt better about himself and regained his confidence; he joined groups and sports teams to try new things, and his failures did not stop him. After shifting his perspective, Jake pursued his aspirations without fear and gradually started to grow better.

After graduating high school, Jake was a confident young man. He received college funds and studied computer science because he loved technology. Jake's story shows how a development mindset can improve one's life and how vital it is to trust oneself even when things go wrong.

What You Should Do:

You now have everything you need to adopt and use a growth attitude. Here's what you should do next:

1. Promise to use the tenets of the growth mindset every day: You should try to follow the rules in this book every day. Be positive about obstacles, see mistakes as chances to learn, and believe in your ability to improve. Take care of your skills and be patient and kind to yourself.

2. If this book spoke to you and provided helpful information, please send it to family, friends, and coworkers who could also benefit from its ideas. Share these growth mindset techniques with others to help them reach their full potential.

3. Your opinion is critical to us. If this book has helped you, please write an honest review on Amazon so others can find these life-changing ideas.

Final Words:

Now that you understand these concepts, have confidence in the process and commit to achieving your full potential. Those who are prepared to embark on this journey will have a promising future. Adhere to these guidelines closely and view every challenge as an opportunity to learn and grow. Now, take action and improve your life as well as the lives of those around you!

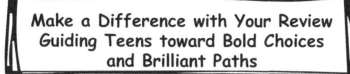

Make a Difference with Your Review
Guiding Teens toward Bold Choices
and Brilliant Paths

"Personal and professional growth is how you unlock your potential. Create a more fulfilling and successful life, full of purpose and resilience."

-Gallagher

People who give without expectation live longer, happier lives and make more money. So, if we've got a shot at that during our time together, darn it, I'm gonna try.

To make that happen, I have a question for you...
Would you help someone you've never met, even if you never got credit for it?

Who is this person, you ask? They are like you—or, at least, like you used to be—less experienced, wanting to make a difference, and needing help but not sure where to look.

Our mission? To make skills of making bold decisions and discovering new career paths to everyone. That's the driving force behind everything I do. And the only way we can achieve that is by reaching out to... well, everyone!

This is where you come in. We often judge a book by its cover (and its reviews), right? So, on behalf of a struggling teen, you've never met:
Could you do us a solid by leaving a review for this book?
It'll take you less than a minute and won't cost a dime, but it could completely turn around a fellow teen's life. Your review might:

- Help a teen learn the art of public speaking.
- Make them step outside of their comfort zone in order to grow.
- Support a student in making the right choice in their career.
- Spark a transformation in a teen's life.
- Make one more dream coZme true.

To get that "feel good" feeling and help this person for real, all you have to do is...and it takes less than 60 seconds...

Leave a review!

Simply scan the QR code below to leave your review:
https://www.amazon.com/review/
review-your-purchases/?asin=BOOKASIN\

Feeling good about helping an anonymous teen? You are exactly my kind of person. Welcome to the club. You're one of us.

Thank you from the bottom of my heart.

Your biggest fan,
Emma.

Leave a review

ABOUT THE AUTHOR

EMMA DAVIS is a woman who wears many hats. She is a clinical social worker, a therapist, and a financial advisor, as well as the author of Effective Anger Management for Teens.

Her books are aimed at teenagers, covering a diverse range of topics, including life and coping skills, DBT techniques, finances, puberty, developing a growth mindset, and career planning. She focuses on the unique challenges faced by adolescents in their emotional and physiological development, empowering readers with a strong foundation for understanding.

Emma draws on experience and knowledge from all her roles, as well as her experience as a mother, to guide young people through the difficult stage of adolescence. She runs a therapy practice and financial education agency tailored to teenagers, and has worked with a diverse range of young people facing different practical and emotional challenges. She also runs several online courses on cultivating interpersonal skills, gratitude, happiness, and joy, as well as 10 residential care facilities for adults with disabilities and mental health challenges, which also informs her work.

Emma is married with 9 children between the ages of 3 and 22. She enjoys spending time with her family, practicing jiu jitsu, and developing her skills in photography.

Helping Teens With Finances, Anger Management, Mental Health, And Future Life Planning

From

EMMA DAVIS

Available on Amazon or wherever books are sold

To learn more about helping teens with finances, anger management, mental health, and future life planning at www.emmadavisbooks.com

BIBLIOGRAPHY

Abdou, A. (2023). 10 Great Personal Development Goals to Set For Yourself & How To Achieve Them. Hive. https://hive.com/blog/personal-development-goals/

aparto . (2023). Top 20 Tips to Study Smarter Not Harder. Apartostudent. https://apartostudent.com/blog/how-to-study-smarter

Best, J. (2020). 4 Ways to Foster A Growth Mindset In Your Classroom. 3plearning. https://www.3plearning.com/blog/4-ways-flick-switch-fixed-growth-mindset-students/

Bradley, J. (2023). Embracing Self-Compassion: Nurturing Yourself in the Journey of Transformation. Johnbradley1. https://johnbradley1.medium.com/embracing-self-compassion-nurturing-yourself-in-the-journey-of-transformation-328297763da4

Building trust through vulnerability [7 ways]. (2024). Zoetalentsolutions. https://zoetalentsolutions.com/building-trust-through-vulnerability/

Burns, M. (2016). Combining a growth mindset and self-compassion for powerful results. Attorneywithalife. https://www.attorneywithalife.com/combining-a-growth-mindset-and-self-compassion-for-powerful-results/

Carla . (2020). How to Influence Your Peers: I'm Winning, but Not Making Any Progress. Maxwellleadership. https://www.maxwellleadership.com/blog/how-to-influence-your-peers-winning-but-not-making-progress/

CARRINGTON , I. (2022). Growth Mindset P owth Mindset Pedagogy and Intr edagogy and Introductory Communication y Communication . Opensiuc. https://opensiuc.lib.siu.edu/cgi/viewcontent.cgi?article=2509&context=gs_rp

Clement, Z. (2020). How to use a growth mindset to improve the quality of your relationships. Mybestself101. https://www.mybestself101.org/blog/2020/6/30/how-to-use-a-growth-mindset-to-improve-the-quality-of-your-relationships

Concept and Principles of Growth and Development. (2023). Educationminder. https://www.educationminder.com/2023/04/Concept-principles-of-growth-and-development.html

Cornélio, A. M., Bittencourt-Navarrete, R. E. de , Brum, R. de B., Queiroz, C. M., & Costa, M. R. (2016). Human Brain Expansion during Evolution Is Independent of Fire Control and Cooking. Ncbi. https://www.ncbi.nlm.nih.gov/pmc/articles/PMC4842772/

Crafting goals aligned with your values. (n.d.). Esoftskills. https://esoftskills.com/crafting-goals-aligned-with-your-values-a-guide/

Davis, T. (2019). 15 Ways to Build a Growth Mindset. Click-Here-Happiness. https://www.psychologytoday.com/us/blog/click-here-happiness/201904/15-ways-build-growth-mindset

Debevoise, N. D. (2019). How Impact, Meaning, And Purpose Are Different (And Why You Should Care). Forbes. https://www.forbes.com/sites/nelldebevoise/2019/12/10/how-impact-meaning-and-purpose-are-different-and-why-you-should-care/?sh=6f8da06f57f2

Developing a Growth Mindset. (n.d.). Learnlife. https://www.learnlife.com/learning-paradigm/developing-a-growth-mindset

Developing a Growth Mindset. (n.d.). Learnlife. https://www.learnlife.com/learning-paradigm/developing-a-growth-mindset

Durden, T. (n.d.). 7 Factors That Influence Your Mindset. Fearlessbusinessboss. https://fearlessbusinessboss.com/7-factors-that-influence-your-mindset/

Education. (2023). Helpful tips to study smarter, not harder. Educanada. https://www.educanada.ca/blog-blogue/2023/study-smarter-etudier-intelligent.aspx?lang=eng

FIGUEROA, R. (2022). Business Growth Through Strategic Business Partnerships: Where to Start. Hingemarketing. https://

hingemarketing.com/blog/story/business-growth-through-strategic-business-partnerships-where-to-start

Fostering Growth Mindset: A Comprehensive Strategy for Student Success. (n.d.). Futureeducationmagazine. https://futureeducationmagazine.com/fostering-growth-mindset-strategy/

Freeman, C. (2023). Being kind to yourself: the importance of self-compassion and patience during healing. Momentaryhappiness. https://momentaryhappiness.com/blogs/news/being-kind-to-yourself-the-importance-of-self-compassion-and-patience-during-healing

futurelearn. (2022). What is a growth mindset and how can you develop one? Futurelearn. https://www.futurelearn.com/info/blog/general/develop-growth-mindset

Galicia, P. L. -, Hernández, M. E. C. -, Mata, F., Mata-Luévanos, J., Serrano, L. M. R. -, Tapia-de-Jesús, A., & Buenrostro-Jáuregui, M. H. (2021). Adult Neurogenesis: A Story Ranging from Controversial New Neurogenic Areas and Human Adult Neurogenesis to Molecular Regulation. Ncbi. https://www.ncbi.nlm.nih.gov/pmc/articles/PMC8584254/

Ganesh, K. (2023). Why is the purpose at work important in the modern workplace? Culturemonkey. https://www.culturemonkey.io/employee-engagement/purpose-at-work/

GGI. (2024). Goal Setting for Success: Empower Yourself to Set and Achieve Goals. Graygroupintl. https://www.graygroupintl.com/blog/goal-setting-for-success

Gilpatrick, Dr. M. (2024). Why Is a Growth Mindset Important in the Classroom? Gcu. https://www.gcu.edu/blog/teaching-school-administration/why-growth-mindset-important-in-classroom

Gilpatrick, Dr. M., Vasquez, T., & Pottinger, E. (2024). Why Is a Growth Mindset Important in the Classroom? Gcu. https://www.gcu.edu/blog/teaching-school-administration/why-growth-mindset-important-in-classroom

gloveworx. (2017). Growth Mindset to Reach Goals. Gloveworx. https://www.gloveworx.com/blog/growth-mindset-goals/

Growth is Essential for Relationships to Thrive. (n.d.). Family-mediationgroup. https://www.familymediationgroup.ca/blog/growth-is-essential-for-relationships-to-thrive

Growth Mindset & Social Emotional Learning. (2022). Scratch-garden. https://scratchgarden.com/blog/growth-mindset-social-emotional-learning/

Growth Mindset. (2024). Tll. https://tll.mit.edu/teaching-resources/inclusive-classroom/growth-mindset/

Growth Mindset: A Teacher's Guide. (2022). Structural. https://www.structural-learning.com/post/growth-mindset-a-teachers-guide

Growth Mindset: What it is, and how to cultivate one. (2024). Oregonstate. https://success.oregonstate.edu/learning/growth-mindset

Hadari, R. (2022). 30 Continuous Improvement Quotes To Motivate Your Team. Goretro. https://www.goretro.ai/post/continuous-improvement-quotes

Hampton , T. (2024). How You Can Use A Growth Mindset To Achieve Your Goals. Takenyahampton. https://takenyahampton.com/how-you-can-use-a-growth-mindset-to-achieve-your-goals/

Harris, H. (2023). How to Prioritize Self-Care and Your Mental Health. Nivati. https://www.nivati.com/blog/how-to-prioritize-self-care-and-your-mental-health

Helvacılar, A. (2023). Nurturing Skills For Success. Sertifier. https://sertifier.com/blog/nurturing-skills-for-success/

Herrity, J. (2023). How to Develop Your Skill Set to Advance Your Career. Indeed. https://www.indeed.com/career-advice/career-development/how-to-develop-your-skill-set

herrity, J. (2024). 7 Ways To Improve Your Personal Development Skills. Indeed. https://www.indeed.com/career-advice/career-development/improve-your-personal-development-skills

HIMELSTEIN, S. (n.d.). 3 Steps to Build Resilience and Practice Self-Care for Helping Professionals in Uncertain Times. Centerforadolescentstudies. https://centerforadolescentstudies.

com/3-steps-to-build-resilience-and-practice-self-care-in-un-certain-times/

How Do Hobbies and Skills Contribute to Your Career and Transitions? (2023). Ashg. https://www.ashg.org/publications-news/trainee-newsletter/how-hobbies-and-skills-contribute-to-your-career-and-transitions/

How to help students develop a growth mindset. (2022). Good-Grief.org. https://good-grief.org/ways-to-develop-a-growth-mindset/

How To Maintain a Healthy Lifestyle: 9 Tips. (2021). Openup. https://openup.com/self-guided-care/blog/how-to-maintain-a-healthy-lifestyle-9-tips/

Huskanović, A. (2023). Why Friends Who Don't Aim High Could Ruin Your Life. Medium. https://medium.com/@ahuskano/why-friends-who-dont-aim-high-could-ruin-your-life-e554f25a6204

Importance of Self-Reflection for Growth Mindset. (n.d.). Changenfocus.

It's Time to Go Beyond Fixed and Growth Mindsets. (n.d.). Soundingboardinc. https://www.soundingboardinc.com/blog/beyond-fixed-and-growth-mindsets/

Jaya. (2023). Developing a Growth Mindset: Unlocking Your Full Potential. Thefluentlife. https://thefluentlife.com/content/developing-growth-mindset/

Khan, S. A. (n.d.). How to practice self-care and build resilience for better mental health Read more at: https://yourstory.com/2023/06/practicing-self-care-building-resilience-mental-health. Yourstory. https://yourstory.com/2023/06/practicing-self-care-building-resilience-mental-health

Kim, Dr. (2020). Self-Compassion and the Growth Mindset. Drkimcorson. https://drkimcorson.com/selfcompassion-and-growth-mindset/

Klieman, K. (n.d.). The Impact of the Growth Mindset. Socialstudies. https://www.socialstudies.com/blog/the-impact-of-the-growth-mindset/

Kristin . (n.d.). Developing a Growth Mindset for Reading. Msjordanreads.https://msjordanreads.com/developing-growth-mindset-reading/

Labrecque, K. (2021). Reaching your full potential isn't out of reach: 10 tips to get moving. Betterup. https://www.betterup.com/blog/full-potential

Lee, S. (2021). The importance of a growth mindset to development. Torch. https://torch.io/blog/the-importance-of-a-growth-mindset-to-development/

LEIKVOLL, V. (n.d.). 20 Life-Changing Personal Development Goals. Leaders. https://leaders.com/articles/personal-growth/personal-development-goals/

LeMaster, J. (2023). Alternative Ways for Measuring Progress and Growth in Reading Assessments. Literacygeeks. https://literacygeeks.com/geek-gazette/2023/10/alternative-ways-for-measuring-progress-and-growth-in-reading-assessments

Liotta, A. (2021). Encourage Students to Embrace a Growth Mindset. Commonlit. https://www.commonlit.org/blog/encourage-students-to-embrace-a-growth-mindset-852cdb0e6d3e/

Living Up To Our Full Potential. (2006). Scotthyoung. https://www.scotthyoung.com/blog/2006/03/24/living-up-to-our-full-potential/

Livneh, S. E. (2021). #GrowthSnacks: Practice your Growth Mindset and Continous Learning In Professional Communities. Growthsnacks. https://growthsnacks.medium.com/growthsnacks-practice-your-growth-mindset-and-continous-learning-in-professional-communities-d36a21c040a8

lovinglifeclinics. (2023). How to Adopt a Growth Mindset & Reach Your Goals. Lovinglifeclinics. https://lovinglifeclinics.com/how-to-adopt-a-growth-mindset-reach-your-goals/

Ludden, D. (2021). Does Personal Growth Benefit a Relationship? Psychologytoday. https://www.psychologytoday.com/au/blog/talking-apes/202103/does-personal-growth-benefit-relationshi

Lyons, P. (2024). 6 reasons why you're not reaching your full potential. Wellnessdaily. https://www.wellnessdaily.com.au/expert/6-reasons-why-you-re-not-reaching-your-full-potential

Making a Plan for Growth Mindset Culture Shift. (n.d.). Mindsetworks. https://www.mindsetworks.com/schools/getting-started

MARELISA. (n.d.). 16 Personal Development Goals That Will Make You Happier and Sexier. Daringtolivefully. https://daringtolivefully.com/personal-development-goals

Marschall, A. (2023). How to Deal With Rejection. Verywellmind. https://www.verywellmind.com/how-to-deal-with-rejection-7260048

Mathews, S. (n.d.). The 10 Important Principles Of Growth And Development Of A Child. Childhood. https://childhood.in/principles-of-growth-and-development-of-a-child/

McGinnis, K. (2022). 5 Ways to Continue Your Skills Development and Grow Your Career. Builtin. https://builtin.com/articles/skills-development

MILLER, A. (n.d.). Six Essential Practices to Improve Listening Skills in Relationships. Estherperel. https://www.estherperel.com/blog/six-essential-practices-to-improve-listening-skills-in-relationships

Miller, K. D. (2020). 5+ Ways to Develop a Growth Mindset Using Grit & Resilience. Positivepsychology. https://positivepsychology.com/5-ways-develop-grit-resilience/

Mindset, G. (2023). Creating A Growth Mindset In The Classroom: 10 Strategies And Fun Activities For Students. Strobeleducation. https://strobeleducation.com/blog/creating-a-growth-mindset-in-the-classroom/

Mosunic, Dr. C. (n.d.). How to improve interpersonal skills in the workplace. Calm. https://www.calm.com/blog/how-to-improve-interpersonal-skills

Nave, K.-A., & Werner, H. B. (2024). Myelination of the nervous system: mechanisms and functions. Pubmed. https://pubmed.ncbi.nlm.nih.gov/25288117/

Neuroplasticity 101. (2024). Brainfutures.org. https://www.brainfutures.org/neuroplasticity-101/

O'Keefe, B. (2011). 5 Steps to Better School/Community Collaboration. Edutopia. https://www.edutopia.org/blog/school-community-collaboration-brendan-okeefe

Overcoming Fear of Rejection. (n.d.). Uncovercounseling. https://uncovercounseling.com/blog/overcoming-fear-of-rejection/

Overcoming Obstacles To Achieve Goals. (2022). Educatorforever. https://www.educatorforever.com/blog/overcoming-obstacles

Parker-Pope, T. (2023). The growth mindset: Why friends, family and work make a difference. Thepost. https://www.thepost.co.nz/wellbeing/350022551/growth-mindset-why-friends-family-and-work-make-difference

Penn , A. (2020). How to Build Healthy Friendships: Get a Growth Mindset. Shortform. https://www.shortform.com/blog/healthy-friendships/

Persevere Through Setbacks And Continue Moving Forward. (n.d.). Fastercapital. https://fastercapital.com/topics/persevere-through-setbacks-and-continue-moving-forward.html

Powerful Communication: Enhancing Skills for Business Masters. (2024). Pepperdine. https://bschool.pepperdine.edu/blog/posts/powerful-communication-enhancing-skills-for-business-masters.htm

Pradeepa, S. (2023). How Do You Overcome Obstacles in Achieving Goals: 15 Keys. Believeinmind. https://www.believeinmind.com/self-growth/how-do-you-overcome-obstacles-in-achieving-goals/

Pratama, I. (2017). 21 Examples of Personal Development Goals for a Better You. Iosipratama. https://iosipratama.medium.com/21-examples-of-personal-development-goals-for-a-better-you-7dddcbc2f1b1

Prieur, J. (2022). 10 Ways Teachers Can Instill a Growth Mindset in Students. Prodigygame. https://www.prodigygame.com/main-en/blog/growth-mindset-in-students/

Principles of Human Growth and Development. (n.d.). Psychol-ogydiscussion. https://www.psychologydiscussion.net/educa-tional-psychology/principles-of-human-growth-and-develop-ment/1813

Prioritizing Yourself: 7 Simple Ways to Incorporate Self-Care. (n.d.). Jodymichael. https://www.jodymichael.com/blog/priori-tizing-7-ways-incorporate-self-care/

Risser, M. (n.d.). Fear of Rejection: Signs, Effects, & How to Over-come. Choosingtherapy. https://www.choosingtherapy.com/fear-of-rejection/

Roychowdhury, D. D. (n.d.). How to develop a growth mindset and achieve your goals. Drdevroy. https://www.drdevroy.com/how-to-develop-growth-mindset/

Sager, J. (2023). 11 Growth Mindset Strategies That Help Your Stu-dents Grow as Learners. Teachstarter. https://www.teachstart-er.com/us/blog/growth-mindset-strategies-to-help-your-stu-dents-grow-as-learners/

Sager, J. (2023). 11 Growth Mindset Strategies That Help Your Stu-dents Grow as Learners. Teachstarter. https://www.teachstart-er.com/us/blog/growth-mindset-strategies-to-help-your-stu-dents-grow-as-learners/

Self Reflection: The Journey of Personal Insight and Growth. (2024). Graygroupintl. https://www.graygroupintl.com/blog/self-reflec-tion

Setting goals for success with a growth mindset. (2022). Apm. https://apm.net.au/employers/employer-resources/setting-goals-for-success-with-a-growth-mindset

Shaping Destinies: The Power of Career Goal Alignment. (2024). Riversoftware. https://www.riversoftware.com/uncategorized/shaping-destinies-the-power-of-career-goal-alignment/

shopipswich. (2024). Adopting a Growth Mindset when Set-ting Goals. Shopipswich. https://www.shopipswich.com.au/news/20-adopting-a-growth-mindset-when-setting-goals

SIU, E. (n.d.). Business Growth Strategies: Optimizing Partnerships for Success. Singlegrain. https://www.singlegrain.com/blog/ms/business-growth-strategies/

Smith, J. (2020). Growth Mindset vs Fixed Mindset: How what you think affects what you achieve. Mindsethealth. https://www.mindsethealth.com/matter/growth-vs-fixed-mindset

Smith, J. (2020). Growth Mindset vs Fixed Mindset: How what you think affects what you achieve. Mindsethealth. https://www.mindsethealth.com/matter/growth-vs-fixed-mindset

Smithyman, T. (n.d.). How to handle rejection. Psyche. https://psyche.co/guides/how-to-handle-rejection-so-that-you-can-heal-and-move-on

Stegall , D. (2023). The Connection Between Growth Mindset and Healthy Lifestyle. Livinghealthylist. https://livinghealthylist.com/personal-development/positive-mindset/the-connection-between-growth-mindset-and-healthy-lifestyle/

success, pathway. (2023). 40+ Strategies and Supports for Students Who Are Failing Class. Thepathway2success. https://www.thepathway2success.com/40-strategies-and-supports-for-students-who-are-failing-class/

Sutton, J. (2021). 18 Best Growth Mindset Activities, Worksheets, and Questions. Positivepsychology. https://positivepsychology.com/growth-mindset/

Tan, K. (2024). How to achieve your full potential. Wikihow. https://www.wikihow.com/Achieve-Your-Full-Potential

Tay, L. (2021). Growth Mindsets in our Relationships. Purdue. https://www.purdue.edu/stepstoleaps/new/featured/well-being-tips/2021/2021_1206.php

The Effect of Growth Mindset on Adolescents' Meaning in Life: The Roles of Self-Efficacy and Gratitude. (2023). Dovepress. https://www.dovepress.com/the-effect-of-growth-mindset-on-adolescents-meaning-in-life-the-roles--peer-reviewed-fulltext-article-PRBM

The Importance of After School Clubs & What Makes a Good One. (2022). Learningcubs. https://www.learningcubs.co.uk/

resources/the-importance-of-after-school-clubs-what-makes-a-good-one

The role of partnerships in growth marketing strategy. (2023). Abmatic. https://abmatic.ai/blog/role-of-partnerships-in-growth-marketing-strategy

Thomas, D. A. (2023). Growth Mindset Success: Tracking Your Progress. Medium. https://medium.com/@DebraAThomasMBA/growth-mindset-success-tracking-your-progress-ca1fe6c-6cd27

Thorpe, D. (2023). Achieving success through purposeful action: why moving with intent matters. Dougthorpe. https://dougthorpe.com/achieving-success-through-purposeful-action-why-moving-with-intent-matters/

Tools , M. (n.d.). Personal Goal Setting. Mindtools. https://www.mindtools.com/a5ykiuq/personal-goal-setting

Top 10 tips on how to study smarter, not longer. (2023). Snexplores. https://www.snexplores.org/article/top-10-tips-study-smarter-not-longer-study-skills

Want to reach your full potential? Know your strengths and weaknesses. (2024). Sngular. https://www.sngular.com/insights/91/want-to-reach-your-full-potential-know-your-strengths-and-weaknesses

What is a growth mindset and how can you develop one? (2022). Futurelearn. https://www.futurelearn.com/info/blog/general/develop-growth-mindset

What is a growth mindset and how can you develop one? (2022). Futurelearn. https://www.futurelearn.com/info/blog/general/develop-growth-mindset

What is a growth mindset and how can you develop one? (2022). Futurelearn. https://www.futurelearn.com/info/blog/general/develop-growth-mindset

Why is reading especially important for teens? (2023). Researchgate. https://www.scottishbooktrust.com/articles/why-is-reading-especially-important-for-teens

Wool, M. (2021). 13 tips to develop a growth mindset. Betterup. https://www.betterup.com/blog/growth-mindset

Wooll, M. (2022). Own your personal development: self-improvement goals that motivate. Betterup. https://www.betterup.com/blog/goals-for-self-improvement

"What'd You Say?" Eight Ways to Listen Better. (2015). Goskybound. https://goskybound.com/eight-ways-to-listen-better/

Your Greatest Ally: A Growth Mindset. (2020). Thesocialleadershipcoach. https://thesocialleadershipcoach.com/your-greatest-ally-growth-mindset/

Zhang, J., Kuusisto, E., Nokelainen, P., & Tirri, K. (2020). Peer Feedback Reflects the Mindset and Academic Motivation of Learners. Frontiersin. https://www.frontiersin.org/articles/10.3389/fpsyg.2020.01701

101+ inspiring growth mindset quotes for kids to fuel their success. (n.d.). Lemonadeday. https://lemonadeday.org/blog/growth-mindset-quotes-for-kids

11 Ways to Develop Skills and Knowledge for Work. (2022). Mbopartners. https://www.mbopartners.com/blog/how-manage-small-business/how-to-keep-your-skills-and-knowledge-current-and-why-it-matters1/

4 Tips for Finding the Right Growth Partner. (n.d.). Startupgrind. https://www.startupgrind.com/blog/4-tips-for-finding-the-right-growth-partner/

5 Examples of Personal Development Goals. (2023). Humanfocus. https://humanfocus.co.uk/blog/5-examples-of-personal-development-goals/

6 simple ways to feel comfortable with rejection. (2019). Conflictexpert. https://the-conflictexpert.com/2019/05/28/the-truth-about-rejection-6-way-to-manage-it-better-and-stop-conflict-from-escalating/

6 Tips to Help Students Develop a Growth Mindset in the Classroom. (2017). Lexialearning. https://www.lexialearning.com/blog/6-tips-help-students-develop-growth-mindset-classroom

6 Ways to Easily Develop Your Skills and Knowledge. (n.d.). Push-far. https://www.pushfar.com/article/6-ways-to-easily-develop-your-skills-and-knowledge/

7 ways to improve your listening skills. (2022). Futurelearn. https://www.futurelearn.com/info/blog/general/7-ways-improve-your-listening-skills

9 Ways to Develop a Growth Mindset in Children through Goal-Setting. (2024). Mulberrylearning. https://mulberrylearning.com/9-ways-to-develop-a-growth-mindset-in-children-through-goal-setting/